PRECIOUS CARGO

The history of the U.S. Army
146th Quartermaster Truck Company

By

Richard T. Bass

This edition published 1993 by Lee Publishing
PO Box 66 EXETER Devon EX2 5FE

ISBN 0 9518934 1 6 Precious Cargo (pbk)

Cover design by Richard J. Whymark

Typesetting by James A. Garrity

Printed and bound by Short Run Press Ltd, Exeter, Devon.

CONTENTS

FOREWORD

In the history of the Second World War support operations of combat units is very often overlooked or ignored to concentrate on front line troops who either succeed at great sacrifice or fail gloriously whilst executing a tactical mission or campaign.

It is often taken for granted that combat troops were adequately provisioned with food, fuel and ammunition during those operations and it is only when a deficiency of this service is highlighted that thought is given as to why or how it has occurred, invariably turning critical attention to the vital role of transport and supply, for without an efficient and effective line of supply any military initiative is doomed to failure.

But someone had the thankless task of driving overloaded trucks for mile after mile over inadequate and war damaged roads, often under fire, from loading points far to the rear of the fighting often right up to the front line.

This true story is of one such unit, based upon surviving archive material, personal documents, and most importantly, the recollections of those men who lived this history, for without their memories it would not be complete.

It is a tribute not only to the men of the 146th but to all their sister units who often in the face of adversity and hardship quietly went about their duty which contributed significantly to the ultimate victory of the Allied forces over the Axis powers.

In 1942 as the newly mobilised U.S. Army adapted and streamlined their peacetime divisions in anticipation of locking horns with Hitler's model army the 146th Quartermaster Truck Company was an almost incidental creation of that necessary organisational reaction to the brutally effective German tactic of "Blitzkrieg" that was being ruthlessly demonstrated across the European continent.

The 146th' pedigree was born of the 29th "Blue and Gray" Infantry Division, a National Guard unit of volunteers from Washington D.C. and the surrounding states. From their very formation in early 1942 from companies of the 104th Quartermaster Regiment to their eventual disbandment in 1946, the 146th enjoyed a unique status of independence from the normal military structure of accountability to a permanent parent unit.

Upon formation they had only a brief history, few customs but no battle honours or traditions to uphold, so they made their own as they slogged their way across two vast continents. From the searing white landscape of the Western Desert, to a brief, bitter sweet encounter with the green of England before crossing the grey waters of the English Channel to France and the slaughter of early summer among the lush fields and orchards of Normandy, through Autumn mud and the panic of the icy Ardennes winter into the black heart of Germany, only stopping once they had entered the gates of Berlin.

These soldiers of the 146th have not attracted or sought the fame, glamour or attention rightly given to famous fighting units - but they were there. They won their battle stars and wrote their own history, which even today - some fifty years on - is reflected upon with pride and affection by all who served in the 146th Quartermaster Truck Company, and is perfectly summarised by one of their number, Berger Bankston.

"All of us who served in the 146th are damned proud of our service, we don't feel the least bit less of a hero because we were in a Quartermaster Truck Company than we would have if we'd been in the infantry, and I think that as a Truck Company we probably saw more enemy action through air raids and strafing than many front line infantry companies did. We did our part, we did it proudly and I think it's very important to note that fifty years after the war so many of us who still survive get together once a year and have a reunion through pure love for one another which was established during an exciting period of our lives that we wouldn't want to go through again probably but we wouldn't take a million dollars for the experience that we had."

Precious Cargo

ACKNOWLEDGEMENT

Every soldier has a story to tell - but modesty, or the belief that it would be of interest to no-one outside his own circle of contemporaries, often prevents personal recollections ever being discovered, innocently keeping dormant some of the most interesting and truthful insights of war.

So it was with the men of the 146th Quartermaster Truck Company until Fred Kennel wrote an article in "Chin Strap" - a 29th Division Association publication - that sparked my interest and resulted in some vigorous correspondence.

As I was introduced to one member after another it became obvious that these veterans of a war almost half a century old still enjoyed and cherished the warm, close bonds of friendship forged so many years before.

Once assured their recollections were indeed worthy of recording I received nothing but unstinting co-operation, help and guidance from them all in compiling a complete history of their unit.

Many archive documents simply weren't available - some accidentally destroyed, others disposed of as a matter of bureaucratic routine - but those that could be found were usually unearthed by Bill Albright whose tenacity in doing so was well rewarded.

Private documents and photographs were given by many, particularly Freddie Cox, Bill Albright, John Axselle, Berger Bankston, Fred Kennel and Rudy Weber.

Personal memories were also freely given by all those former members of the 146th that could be traced including Karl Bearscove, Louis Brienza, Jim Brown, Garland Coghill, Chris Controwinski, Glenn McIlwee, Gaylon Priest, Danny Sillers, Abraham Yaffe and Mike Zemel.

One curious fact emerged to the astonishment of everyone when it was discovered that during all their post war reunions no-one ever discussed or even raised the subject of what was probably their saddest assignment - hauling bodies from the infamous Exercise "Tiger".

Their corroborated evidence of this contentious episode is therefore fresh and illuminating, dispelling rumours and guesses that for years have been accepted as truth.

Credit for this book is entirely due to the 146th Quartermaster Truck Company veterans, every one of whom has enthusiastically shared their youthful wartime experiences, given encouragement and offered sound advice.

It proved impossible to trace many veterans to gather their recollections but the colourful career and spirit of the 146th is encapsulated within these pages.

There are a few footnotes of sadness too - Freddie Cox died before he could see this book he worked so hard for, and Bill Albright discovered how close he had been living to an untraced 146th veteran, Sam McClelland, only when he read his obituary in a local paper.

CHAPTER ONE

UNEASY PEACE

26th May 1936 - 7th February 1941

Company 'A' were enjoying their Annual Dinner at Burt's Tavern on New York Avenue, Washington D.C. - and they had good reason for celebrating. It was the 6th of July 1938 and in the two years since formation their ranks had swelled to a respectable fifty -five volunteer soldiers, and they were beginning to receive new equipment too - one such occasion even prompting an illustrated article in the "Detroit Times" commemorating the presentation of their new command car from the manufacturer.

The atmosphere throughout dinner was optimistic and light hearted, talk alternating between well-worn tales of individual misfortune guaranteed to provoke roars of laughter, and the future. Horizons which after years of dark economic depression were looking brighter and more promising than ever.

Company 'A', First Battalion, 104th Quartermaster Regiment of the 29th Infantry Division had been organised and Federally recognised as part of the District of Columbia National Guard on 26th May 1936, and had straight away plunged into a series of military initiations.

They attended the 29th Division encampment at Indiantown Gap, Pennsylvania that year. Trained at Camp Ritchie, Maryland in 1937, at Passage Creek, Virginia in 1938, and participated in corps manoeuvres at Manassas, Virginia in 1939. December of that year saw them winter training for a week at Fort Meade, Maryland - a place they would come to know very well indeed.

It was proudly noted in a regimental summary of late 1940 that since their organisation, Company 'A' had sent two men to the National Marksmanship Matches at Camp Perry, Ohio, and one man had been commissioned in the 104th Quartermaster Regiment.

Praise continued for no deficiencies were noted on the annual or camp inspection reports and special mention was made of the Company drivers having covered 35,114 miles at the annual encampment of 1938 without a single accident or mishap.

When Company 'B' was formed in June 1937, the backbone of its enlisted personnel were drawn from Company 'A' whose men also bolstered the ranks of the Headquarters Company and Medical Detachment of the 104th Quartermaster Regiment.

Company 'C', 2nd Battalion was activated at Richmond, Virginia in 1937 as part of the Virginia National Guard and John Axselle was... "one of the founder members of the outfit. I went with the Company Commander and rode all over the state of Virginia. We'd pick up a truck at Charlotteville, bring it back - I was a farm boy, didn't have a regular job so if they wanted to pick up a truck I got a day's pay! - he and I got in a station wagon, go pick up a truck, I'd drive it back to Richmond and man I was getting to see the State of Virginia and never been out of it! 116th Infantry would have a truck and they'd say 'We starting this Truck Company, National Guard outfit. We're gonna take two of your trucks, you'll have to make do with two less' We were repainting them and putting our insignia on them. I remember distinctly went to New York Manoeuvre Area about 1940 and I was riding round on a damned truck with a broomstick, sitting on the spare tyre back of the cab and it had 'tank' written on the side. First army manoeuvres that's all we had - dump trucks for tanks and sticks for guns."

Kenneth R. Munroe had been commissioned as a Second Lieutenant into Company 'A' on the 1st of August 1940 and straight away set off for these very same three-week manoeuvres at Plattsburgh, New York state with Louis Brienza, Dan Sillers, Fred Kennel and John Crandall, all of whom except Kenneth Munroe were to see the unit through all its metamorphic changes almost to deactivation.

By the summer of 1940 changes were already quietly taking place within the 29th Division in anticipation of imminent Federalisation, including the reassessment of personnel.

Robert M. Schaefer who had been with Company 'A' since its earliest days opted to leave the National Guard in June 1940 but at the outbreak of war enlisted with the U.S. Navy.

First Sergeant Keough was over age and had to be replaced, so Captain Cockrell considered his successor, and among the candidates were Sergeant Karl Bearscove and Staff Sergeant Hubert L. Cocke.

Karl had moved in the late 1930's from his home in Seattle to Washington D.C. to work for the Postal Service and had roomed with two men, Weeks and York who between them had persuaded Karl to join them in the 104th QM Regiment. He was qualified to replace Keough because of previous Regular Army experience and Hubert Cocke through his present rank and excellent record as a Guardsman. Both had successfully completed the Army Extension Course - commonly known as the "Ten Series" - and were eligible to be commissioned as Second Lieutenants upon induction in the Army, provided they passed the physical.

Cocke got the job and took over as First Sergeant in December 1940 when the 29th Division of National Guardsmen from Virginia, Maryland, Pennsylvania and the District of Columbia was a conventional army unit of peacetime proportions and organisation.

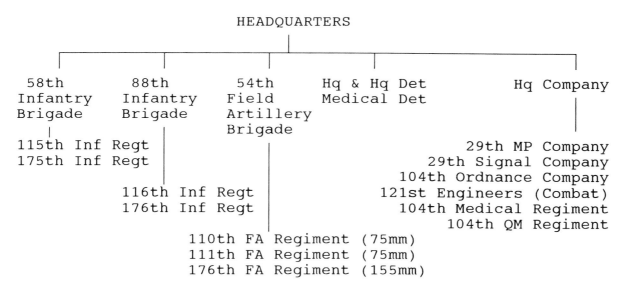

```
            29th INFANTRY DIVISION (1940)

                   HEADQUARTERS
                        |
  ┌─────────┬─────────┬─────────┬──────────────┬──────────────┐
 58th      88th      54th      Hq & Hq Det      Hq Company
Infantry  Infantry   Field     Medical Det           |
Brigade   Brigade    Artillery                        |
   |                 Brigade
115th Inf Regt                            29th MP Company
175th Inf Regt          |               29th Signal Company
              |                       104th Ordnance Company
        116th Inf Regt          121st Engineers (Combat)
        176th Inf Regt           104th Medical Regiment
                      |               104th QM Regiment
          110th FA Regiment (75mm)
          111th FA Regiment (75mm)
          176th FA Regiment (155mm)
```

Source - "Order of Battle U.S. Army, World War II"
         By Selby L. Stanton.

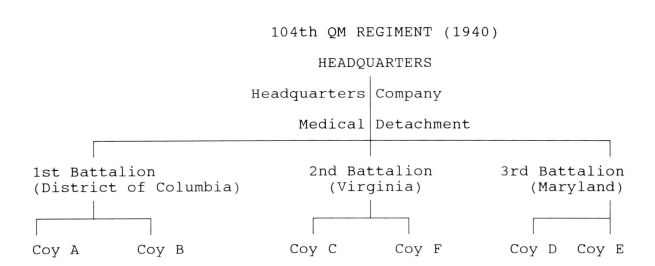

In January 1941 Bearscove and Cocke both submitted to the physical examinations conditional to gaining commissions and Cocke failed because of a spot on his lungs and was sent home. Bearscove was commissioned on 3rd February and sent to a service school of the Adjutant Generals Department, later being reassigned to the Classification and Assignment Section of the Ordnance Replacement Training Centre at Aberdeen Proving Grounds, Maryland.

An ironic ending to this episode is explained by Karl..."By the middle of 1943 I had been promoted to Captain and was Chief of my Section. One evening while serving as Officer of the Day I was inspecting the guard at one of the training companies. The Sergeant of the Guard said that one of the Privates on duty in the guardroom claimed to know me. I entered the room and was confronted by the spectre of ex-First Sergeant Cocke dressed in the ill-fitting uniform of a recruit. Cocke was understandably bitter at the fate which had deprived him of his commission and then ignominiously inducted him into the Army as a Private. The bitterness had transformed him from the spruce soldier he had been to an almost slovenly appearing rookie. A few days later a directive came down which recognised the injustice incurred in cases such as Cocke's. I immediately had him report to my office and advised him of his right to apply for and receive his commission as 2nd Lieutenant. Cocke was at first reluctant to forgive and forget, but he was finally persuaded to submit his application. Cocke accepted his commission and was reassigned. One of the ironies of this story is that in 1947 I was retired for physical disability. The diagnosis was a spot on my lungs."

At the beginning of 1941 the United States had been an interested bystander to the flames of the European conflict and it was the fervent hope of most Americans that they would not become physically involved. But public and political opinion was divided as to just how deeply the United States should become implicated in what some saw as a far off quarrel that did not merit the interference and inevitable sacrifice of young American lives, drawing a parallel to the First World War when American troops had broken the stalemate of European trench warfare by tipping the scales of military might in favour of their Mother Country.

Others supported President Roosevelt's view that American military participation was a sad inevitability and the nation should therefore not only urgently prepare herself, but in the meantime support Winston Churchill and prop up the embattled British Empire through the generous medium of "Lend - Lease".

National Guardsmen were part-time, volunteer soldiers so it was accepted as quite natural and normal for individual companies to be composed almost exclusively of men from the immediate locality of their Company headquarters, resulting in formations of friends, neighbours and relatives all serving in a unit that was bonded by a camaraderie much stronger than anything the military could ever contrive.

The motives of these volunteers for joining the National Guard were many and varied, for as the United States was still reeling from years of economic stagnation it was now confronted by the very real possibility of going to war as Fred Cox remembers only too well... "During 1940 the situation in Europe became much worse. The U.S. instituted conscription to increase the armed forces and new camps were needed fast, so in the Autumn of 1940 my father and two older brothers went to work helping to build one of these camps. I couldn't qualify as a carpenter so I was out of work. In January of 1941 my boyhood chum talked me into joining the National Guard. We decided to do our year of active duty and put it behind us, so when we had a civilian job later we wouldn't have to worry about being drafted at the age of twenty-one."

This mature appreciation of the situation and concern for their future outweighed the detail of being under age to enlist as Berger Bankston recalls... "Well, Freddie and I were both seventeen years old, I was a month and a half younger than he was, and we lied about our age."

Fred... "Told 'em I was born in 1922 instead of 1923 - it just kept it simpler!"

Some were so keen to join the National Guard they went to extraordinary lengths. Fred Kennel remembers... "Louis Brienza's brother had glasses that looked like the bottom of a milk bottle. The guys took him into the 104th Medical Infirmary at night and rehearsed him on the eye chart. He passed that, but the next time he had a physical - he flunked, and cried."

Berger knew some of the men who... "had been in Company 'A' for several years prior to the unit going into Federal service. Louis Brienza was a Staff Sergeant, we had a First Sergeant McLemore, Sergeant Donald Harding, Sergeant John Goodwin and Sergeant Lester Cox. The commander was Captain Henry Cockrell who was a short, rather stout little man, too old for active combat, and a First Sergeant Hubert Cocke who applied for a commission just prior to our going into Federal service."

In the early days Company 'A' was quartered in the D.C. National Guard armoury which was an old hotel called the "National Hotel" on 6th and Pennsylvania Avenue, North West Washington D.C., which Berger Bankston remembers... "was so old that it was known to be a fact that John Wilkes Booth who shot Abraham Lincoln had stayed there on a number of occasions when he was playing on the bill of Fords Theater. Ironically Abraham Lincoln also stayed at that same hotel which the National Guard had taken over as an armoury where each Company was assigned a certain number of rooms, and of course the National Guard was not up to full strength. A Company may have consisted only of twenty or thirty men rather than one hundred and nine which was the later wartime strength. The Company would meet twice a month for what we called 'Drill Night' at which time we would put on our uniforms and gather our equipment, then march single file down the steps, six floors to street level and form up on the sidewalk in front of all the passers-by, then march across Pennsylvania Avenue to a triangle where we would drill."

CHAPTER TWO

Fort George G. Meade, Maryland

8th February - 14th September 1941

12th February 1941:

General Erwin Rommel arrives in Tripoli closely followed by advance detachments of his German expeditionary force. Sent by Hitler to bolster his sagging Italian allies, Rommel's "Afrika Korps" are within six weeks aggressively regaining that territory so eagerly abandoned by their Italian allies during a providential advance by Australian troops. This new German/Italian counter offensive coincides with the hurried despatch of a large force of British Eighth Army troops from North Africa to Greece in an ill-fated attempt to prevent the threatened German invasion through the Balkans from the north.

11th March 1941:

The "Lend-Lease" Bill is passed into law by the narrowest of majorities, opening the way for America to start officially supplying Britain with raw materials, food, weapons and military equipment. Roosevelt not only felt obliged to prop up Britain in the west and prepare for the probable involvement of his own armies in that supporting operation at some time in the near future, but he also had to look over his shoulder at the growing threat from the east - Japan. It was an unenviable position to be in but he was blessed with the foresight that the United States would become involved, transforming a Continental war into global conflict and he was now doing everything possible to prepare his nation for that inevitability. This involved not only the resurrection of dispirited and neglected industrial manufacturers to meet the projected material requirements of Roosevelt's new armies, but also the finding of an immediate source of manpower from which to create those armies - the National Guard was his obvious and only immediate option.

22nd June 1941:

Buoyed by the confidence of his armies seeming invincibility, Hitler unleashes his forces in Operation "Barbarossa" against his uneasy ally, Russia. Initially achieving massive and spectacular successes, the Russian winter will start to bite, compelling the German armies to halt and face a bitter cold war of attrition against an ever growing Red Army.

7th December 1941:

The Japanese mount a ferocious, sneak air attack on the U.S. Pacific Fleet at anchor in Pearl Harbour as their practical declaration of war on the United States and it is this one foul deed that finally unleashes the mighty American war machine to wreak vengeance on the Axis alliance of Japan and Germany.

But this last chapter of uneasy Sino-American relations has yet to be reached and the National Guardsmen of the 104th Quartermaster Regiment can only watch world events and swop predictions as to where it will all lead.

On the 3rd of February 1941 the President of the United States called his National Guard into Federal service on one small step of the United States' journey into the Second World War - for the National Guard it was a momentous leap.

It became a date branded on the memories of men of the 29th Infantry Division as it heralded the beginning of a four and a half year long adventure from which many comrades and friends were never to return.

As a member of that Division, Berger Bankston remembers an almost carnival atmosphere as... "we left Washington D.C. with a great deal of fanfare amid newspaper publicity and motion picture cameras."

It didn't take long for that heady atmosphere to dissipate, and a few days later, with the whole Division, Chris Controwinski, his friends and colleagues in Company 'A' 104th Quartermaster Regiment..."went out to Fort George G. Meade."

The site of Fort Meade had been a Union Army railhead beside the village of Admiral, Maryland during the Civil War and had since served the Army well. Buildings to accommodate nearly 54,000 men were first erected in late 1917 and named Camp Meade after Major General George Gordon Meade who had led Union forces at the battle of Gettysburg.

During the American involvement in the First World War about 103,000 troops were trained here, the camp later served as a demobilization centre welcoming those same soldiers returning from Europe.

To avoid confusion with Fort Meade in South Dakota the camp was renamed Fort Leonard Wood in 1928 when it was made a permanent Army installation, and the following year officially adopted its new and preferred full title of Fort George G. Meade.

By 1941 it had grown into Maryland's fourth largest community covering 13,500 acres and over the next four years was destined to see more than three and a half million men pass through its gates on their way to war.

It was here that the process of bringing the newly mobilised 29th Division to a state of combat readiness was begun for there were many basic deficiencies that had to be urgently addressed, not least of which was how to bring the level of personnel up to strength for it was sadly lacking in numbers.

Training was another vital consideration, and according to Berger Bankston, Company 'A'... "took basic training at Fort Meade. Thirteen weeks with a company which was not up to full strength, getting ready for the drafted men who were later to come in the service. After those initial thirteen weeks of training a cadre was formed which would be used to train the drafted men. "

That chronic shortage of manpower is precisely illustrated by Fred Cox... "When we went to Meade we had approximately twenty-three men, might have been twenty-five or twenty-six but seemed like we didn't have very many. We had to try to do the same thing that normally a hundred men would do. Guard duty, do KP, haul soft coal for the kitchen stoves and coal for the pot-bellied stoves to heat the barracks. Get off at four o'clock, go to barracks and have to shine our shoes and press our clothes, take a shower and shave and five o'clock go for twenty-four hours of guard duty. Then we'd get off the next evening at five o'clock and that night we might have what we called 'Firewatch' when we'd have to tend to the fires in the barracks and the kitchens and the orderly room to keep the fires going. Once you got off guard duty you were supposed to have twenty-four hours free, not necessarily to go into town but you didn't have to make all the formations. So anyway we's trying to do the same job as a hundred men."

Within weeks, groups of bewildered 'draftees' began to arrive at Fort Meade to bring the units up to strength. Fred Cox believes it was... "on 15th April 1941 approximately we received our 'Selectees'. They were men that in September 1940 were twenty-one years of age and they were considered 'Selected' - but technically they were drafted. We got enough of 'em to add up to a hundred and five men in the Company, but first two weeks they were quarantined. After that training began."

Company A, 104th QM Regiment

Rudy Weber was a draftee who arrived... "at Fort Meade and was assigned to the 29th Division. My first three weeks I had basic training with an Anti-Tank company - the only antitank equipment we had were a few stove pipes on wheels, but I did qualify on the M1 rifle as a sharpshooter. One day at 'Retreat' some officers from Division Headquarters went through the ranks and picked out all the short men. Being a shade under five feet five inches I was one of the chosen and that same evening we and our papers were sent to the lower end of camp where we slept on mattresses on the floor of an empty building. In the morning I was assigned to Company 'A' 104th Quartermaster Regiment. Up to this point I had only been issued some fatigues, one summer uniform and a winter overseas cap, shoes and underwear. My first detail was guard duty I had no idea what a guard did or was supposed to know! I washed the only shirt I had and while it was drying got a quick course on guard duties."

The Company 'A' cadre who would see to the training of the draftees was, according to Berger Bankston... "composed of Second Lieutenant George E. Miley, who was a very short, feisty, cocky little man, Sergeant Donald Harding, Sergeant John Goodwin, Corporal Nicholas Babbis and Corporal Berger M. Bankston. It should be noted that Corporal Babbis and I did most of the training, the two sergeants spent a great deal of their time in the barracks playing cards and drinking beer and letting Babbis and I do the work. I had lied about my age when I enlisted and was promoted through Private First Class to Corporal and was training recruits and giving them sex hygiene lectures prior to my eighteenth birthday. After the training cadre was formed, it was put through six weeks of intensive basic training prior to the draftees coming in, and then the recruits were put through thirteen more weeks of basic which meant that Corporal Babbis and I had received more than thirty weeks of basic training! This was exactly the same training as all the infantry regiments of the 29th Division, the only difference is that we were taught how to drive trucks and given first echelon maintenance training."

But not everyone was amenable or inclined to military discipline during training, Berger... "had a man in my squad who was a country boy from down in Indianhead, Maryland, and he didn't like to shave. We had an inspection one Saturday morning and passing that inspection was very important to everybody because we wanted passes for the weekend. We got all ready for the inspection and the Colonel was due in about five minutes - and George Posey hadn't shaved! We weren't able to use the latrine for shaving because it had already been cleaned for the inspection so there was nothing left to do but sit him down on a foot locker and dry shave him with a safety razor."

Parades are an integral part of military life offering participants an opportunity to display what they can do in the form of a practical, morale boosting exercise - which on occasions do not quite live up to expectations as Berger Bankston found out... "after we had completed our training, they wanted the D.C. National Guard to parade in Washington D.C. to show the home folks what we looked like. So we paraded down Constitution Avenue on a Sunday afternoon - the entire 29th Division - and there were just a handful

Berger Bankston

of people walking down the sidewalks who just happened to be in Washington at that time who saw the parade. No-one turned out, and we were so angry because the home town folks didn't turn out to see us."

Glenn McIlwee was also in that disappointing Washington parade... "We had to go into Washington D.C. that day to show everybody our trucks and how we looked driving them. It must have been the hottest day on earth. We had those damned canister gas masks and we had to drive the trucks down Constitution Avenue with those gas masks on! Perspiration ran down inside the masks and leaked out of the bottom."

"On the other hand"... Berger Bankston recalls... "we paraded in Baltimore at nine o'clock at night in a driving downpour of rain and the sidewalks were something like ten to fifteen people deep, waving flags and cheering as we went by, ignoring the rain - so we were quite pleased with the City of Baltimore. We participated in a parade at Fort Meade for the Secretary of War, Henry Stimson, to show him what type of training we had received and how we looked, and the entire division paraded before him to the command of the bugle. The Division's bugler would blow the command, each Regimental bugler would repeat the command on his bugle and the command of execution would be given by the company commanders. It was quite impressive."

Now at full strength and all basically trained, personnel were selected or volunteered for specialisation and several from Company 'A' left Fort Meade to attend courses including Chris Controwinski who... "was lucky and sometime in the summer of 1941 I was assigned to a Quartermaster Mechanics School at Fort Holabird and had a two-month course on general mechanics."

These two-month courses were the consequence of an acute shortage of trained men to maintain the thousands of new vehicles being produced for the Army and three regional Mechanics Schools were established in addition to Fort Holabird all under the control of the Quartermaster General.

Captain James Lyle

Thus a standardised and coordinated programme of training was rapidly achieved for officers and enlisted men, but this situation was only to exist until July 1942 when all the schools were transferred to the Chief of Ordnance.

Fred Cox also took a course... "We had a cook's and baker's school run by the Quartermaster. I went through that school and I received a diploma, gold seal and blue ribbon on it. Says I was a 'First Cook and Baker'. I could boil water without burning it but I couldn't do much better than that!"

Fred's course was part of an Army-wide programme urgently initiated by the Quartermaster Corps to regulate and standardise messing procedures with particular emphasis upon the correct methods of preparation and dispensing of food through trained personnel.

So far the Division had been brought up to strength by the simple process of posting in 'draftees' to the various component units, but re-equipping with more modern weapons, equipment and vehicles presented its own problems, for the nation's manufacturing capability and capacity was still only now creaking hesitantly forward at Roosevelt's insistent goading.

The 104th Quartermaster Regiment had been using 1930's vintage trucks and the time had come to replace them. That's when Berger Bankston and... "many of the drivers of our Company were loaded on three or four trucks and driven from Fort Meade to Pontiac, Michigan, to the factory for the purpose of picking up our new trucks right at the assembly line. On arrival we found out that they were so short of help because of the draft and men going in the service they didn't have enough drivers to drive the trucks off the assembly line, so we remained there for three or four days performing that duty. As a truck would reach the end of the assembly line and the last bit of work was done on it, one of us would get in the cab and drive it off the assembly line out of the building to the parking area, park it and get on a shuttle back to the factory to pick up another truck.

Eventually they determined which trucks would be assigned to us and we formed convoys to proceed back to Fort Meade."

Fred Cox was one of the drivers... "bringing back a lot of trucks and there were enough of us to be divided into several convoys. The first night we stopped over in a field and I slept on the troop seat. Let the troop seat down and laid on it, and I only had one blanket with me. I'd actually brought it to sit on 'cause I'm kinda short. That blanket seemed like it was just too small. Didn't cover all my back or something, every time I moved a little bit, and that damned wooden seat was the hardest thing I ever slept on I believe. The next night we stayed in the armoury in Little Washington, Pennsylvania and so the third day we drove straight on in to Fort Meade."

For some a promising future could be dashed from the most unexpected quarter. Lieutenant Monroe had been appointed as Adjutant of the 2nd Battalion, 104th Quartermaster Regiment... "and was really enjoying my new duties. The next thing I knew I received orders to report to a Medical Board at Walter Reed Hospital."

As a result of that Board's decision he received... "orders sending me home to D.C. I was really broken hearted at this turn of events since I had looked forward to serving with my friends in the 104th QM Regiment. My separation was on March 3, 1941. "

CHAPTER THREE

A.P. Hill Military Reservation, Virginia

18th - 25th September 1941

23rd September 1941:

President Roosevelt announces that the United States is considering arming its merchant vessels against German attack. This public declaration supports his "shoot on sight" order to U.S. warships earlier in the month precipitated by a U-boat attack on the U.S.S. *Greer* engaged on Atlantic convoy protection.

24th September 1941:

Fifteen nations including the United States, Britain and the U.S.S.R. sign the "Atlantic Charter", a document drawn up and agreed to by all signatories that will ease the diplomatic path of the United States to war by declaring the aims of such a war are to preserve other nations rights to be free of foreign pressure.

Although Company 'A' stayed here for only a few days they knew it almost as well as General Ambrose Powell Hill's soldiers who winter - camped here in 1862, for 146th truck convoys had made several visits here already, one in particular Berger Bankston recalls when... "we were used to haul the 44th Division from Fort Dix, New Jersey to A.P. Hill, Virginia."

Fred Cox was with him on that assignment which was also his first trip, helping to... "haul the 44th Division to A.P. Hill, Virginia where they stayed a few days. Then I remember two trips out of A.P. Hill with the old trucks and we went back a third time after we got the new trucks."

Rudy Weber remembers his first trip too... "When I was assigned to Company 'A' I told them I couldn't drive. Answer 'We'll teach you the Army way'. A few months later I was posted for convoy duty to haul troops from Fort Meade to A.P. Hill, Virginia, a trip of about 100 miles on busy highways. Again I told them I couldn't drive and that I'd had no instructions as promised. Sergeant Russell took me to the Motor Pool and explained that 'this is a steering wheel etcetera.' I told him that those things I knew, I just didn't drive! He had me start the engine and drive around the Motor Pool twice and shift gears twice. Quoting Russell, 'Hell, you can drive!' The convoy loaded up with troops and away we went to A. P. Hill. Boy you learn fast! - I eventually learned to drive about every motor vehicle the Army had."

CHAPTER FOUR

North Carolina Manoeuvre Area

29th September - 7th December 1941

3rd October 1941:

Major General Lewis H. Brereton commanding the U.S. Third Air Force had been totally preoccupied with reorganising the maintenance and supply echelons of his command following hard lessons learned during the Louisiana maneuvers where their mission was of operating two maintenance commands in support of the air arms of the two "opposing" forces.

His efforts were directed towards completion of the re-organisation in time for the forthcoming Carolina maneuvers, but in this he was thwarted by his appointment as commander of the Far East Air Forces in the Philippines.

31st October 1941:

A German U-boat sinks the U.S. destroyer *Reuben James* with the loss of one hundred sailors while escorting an Atlantic convoy of unarmed merchantmen laden with "Lend-Lease" supplies. It is an ironic loss now for Allied shipping losses are decreasing every month as German U-boat packs are diverted away from the Atlantic to the Mediterranean.

29th November 1941:

With their carrier force already at sea and sailing for Pearl Harbour, the Japanese government decide that Roosevelt's latest ultimatum demanding their withdrawal from China and Indo-China in return for renegotiated trade deals is unacceptable. Their alternative is to go to war, a decision discussed before Emperor Hirohito who has no power or sway over his minister's decisions and can only give his silent assent.

2nd December 1941:

Japanese naval headquarters transmit a message to their carrier force informing them that negotiations have broken down and the attack on Pearl Harbour is to be executed.

6th December 1941:

Roosevelt sends a final appeal for peace to Hirohito but no reply is received, instead a fourteen-part Japanese radio message to their embassy in Washington is intercepted and decoded, the first thirteen parts being passed rapidly to Roosevelt who correctly interprets them as a preamble to a declaration of war.

7th December 1941:

Decoding of the final part of the Japanese message confirms that relations are being broken off and Japan's Washington embassy are instructed to deliver the whole message to the U.S. government at 13:00 hours - dawn at Pearl Harbour.

Training the National Guard intensified in modern tactics, drills and maneuvers but the only accurate way to assess an individual unit's proficiency was to compare it with another, and the 29th Division was first put to the test when they were sent to the North Carolina Manoeuvre Area to put into practice all they had been taught so far and to be assessed as a fighting unit.

They were to be but a small part of the proposed manouevres for it was the under strength U.S. First Army commanded by Lieutenant General Hugh Drum that were under scrutiny.

The First Army at this time was composed of I Corps (8th, 9th and 30th Infantry Divisions), II Corps (28th, 29th and 44th Infantry Divisions), and VI Corps (1st and 26th Infantry Divisions), all of whom were to participate in manouevres that were divided into three phases.

The 6th to 18th of October was allocated to corps commanders to conduct corps-type training; 20th October to 14th November was to be used by the First Army to conduct three separate manouevres, and the final period between 16th and 30th November was for GHQ directed manouevres.

Berger Bankston went with the 29th Infantry Division to... "Morven, North Carolina with the First Army. Other divisions that maneuvered with them were the 28th, the 26th, 44th and some others. The 28th was sent back to camp in Pennsylvania from Morven for more training because they were considered to be very sloppily trained at that time."

Rudy Weber's recollection of the manouevres highlights a persistent shortage of up to date weapons... "we had about nineteen rifles for guard duty in the Company and we were told to carve guns from wood, but instead we bought kid's toy guns and we had a lot of fun playing with cap pistols. We had little equipment, trucks were used with 'tank' written on the side, everything else we had was from World War I"

The field exercises and mock battles took place in an area of over 7,000 square miles of the Carolinas where the topography varied from swamps to rolling hills and the quality of roads varied from first rate highways to dirt and clay roads, some not much more than woodland trails.

Quite predictably these manouevres were not the most comfortable of field exercises, nearly all personnel being housed under canvas which presented practical problems for Fred Cox when he arrived... "In a field outside of Morven, we had to pick the cotton out the field first and then pitch the tents in pretty sandy soil. The tents! You couldn't hardly drive a tent stake in, the damn thing would lift up and come out."

Rudy Weber

But once the Company area was established a routine emerged, not always to everyone's liking but resolved in typical soldier fashion as witnessed by Berger Bankston... "It was very cold down there in the fall of the year in the mornings. We would fall out for reveille very early, five thirty - six o'clock in a very chilly temperature. Well, we found we would be standing in the company street between the rows of tents waiting for the bugle to blow reveille and waiting the formation when we would receive our instructions for the day. We'd see the horn of Philips' trumpet stuck through the flap of his tent and he would blow reveille. It wasn't hard to determine that Philips had not gotten dressed at all. He just stuck that horn through the flap, blew reveille and went back to bed! Well the men resented that and we had quite a bit of conversation about it, so a couple of our fellows - I believe it was Aubrey Rhea and Bob Bennett - decided to fix him. They got hold of his horn one night while he was away and they stuffed the horn with rags and shoved them down in there as hard as they could. The next morning when we had reveille, everybody was tipped off what was going to happen and we were all standing there waiting. We saw the bell of the horn come through the flap of the tent and all you could hear was a lot of grunting, no music coming out, and an awful lot of curse words. Philips discovered that someone had stuffed his horn with rags and he was furious, wanting to clean up on anybody that did it. Of course nobody would tell and it turned out the only way he could get the rags out of the horn was to put it in a bonfire and burn them out. He swore that horn never had the same tone after that, it didn't sound as good, and I really believe he was correct."

Fred Cox, with the rest of the Company..."stayed down in the Carolinas on maneuvers about two and a half months. We left about 5 o'clock in the morning of 7th December 1941, and drove all day 'til just about darkness. We went to this little country airport near Clarksville, mainly just a big field for private planes - that was the only place big enough to accommodate so many trucks. So we pulled up in lines and getting organised for evening chow, and someone had a battery operated radio,

Ricks, Alvin Bowles & Lester Cox

turned it on and 'Oh man, you hear that! Damned Japs bombed Pearl Harbour!' All I could think about, I had less than two months with the original twenty-three of Company 'A' to go and our year would be up - we planned to get out. Anyway the realisation hit us that we would be at war and didn't know how long the war would last or even if some of us would get killed. That sure ruined that Sunday for me!"

Clarksville, VA

He wasn't the only one - Chris Controwinski had... "finished up my course in Baltimore on Saturday the 6th December. Sunday December the 7th was a day of infamy. I reported back to Fort Meade and we were waiting for the 29th Division with Company 'A' to come back from Carolina maneuvers to our company area. We had a skeleton crew there and they put me on guard duty, I was walking a post at Fort Meade carrying a dummy rifle. That was Sunday evening when I heard about Pearl Harbour and I knew the Division was on the way back. They arrived on Tuesday December the 9th. We were signed up to do a years duty and it was to be up on 3rd February 1942. We were counting the days until we would be out of the service and go back home. Well Pearl Harbour changed all that!"

Glen McIlwee was in the convoy heading back to Fort Meade... "driving the convoy commander, and at his direction I backed the vehicle into a lane leading to a large mansion to check truck spacing. We noticed three women running towards us from the mansion - they gave us the news concerning Pearl Harbour."

Rudy Weber was in the rearguard of that convoy... "and going through Durham, North Carolina a man ran up to the truck with a newspaper about Pearl Harbour."

Maneuvers

CHAPTER FIVE

Fort George G. Meade, Maryland

9th December 1941 - 28th April 1942

8th December 1941:

Having delivered their official declarations of war three hours after their Pearl Harbour attack of 7th December, the Japanese launch invasion operations the following day against the Philippines, Malaya and Hong Kong. Opening with attacks on airfields they effectively destroyed all the defending aircraft on the ground, allowing their amphibious landings to be made almost unopposed.

22nd December 1941:

Roosevelt and Churchill meet in Washington at the "Arcadia Conference" where the policy of defeating Germany before Japan is confirmed, and where it is further agreed that to achieve this there must be a massive build up of U.S. military might in Britain for future land operations against Germany.

30th December 1941:

In the North African desert Allied armies suffer severe losses while pursuing the "Afrika Korps", discovering their fighting spirit and discipline is quite different to that of the Italians they are used to engaging. Even as Rommel retreats he is secretly planning a New Year counter attack with tanks that are now arriving, unaware that he will be able to exploit British weak points to such an extent that his counter attack will escalate into a full scale advance eastwards.

13th January 1942:

German U-boats begin operating off the east coast of the United States sinking 150,000 tons of shipping in the first month of their Operation "Drum Roll", increasing their success in February and again in March they extend operations to include waters off South Africa.

28th April 1942:

Japanese forces in the Far East are pressing their advantage in all campaigns with startling success. Seemingly unstoppable their shock tactics of surprise so effectively employed against Pearl Harbour are repeatedly proving effective against Allied forces who are unable even to contain them.

Fred Cox arrived back at Fort Meade where... "everything was all confusion for the next few days. President Roosevelt declared war on the Japs, the Axis declared war on the U.S., then the U.S. declared war on the Axis, and right away we started hauling troops of the 29th Division to patrol the shoreline of Maryland and Virginia!"

Rudy Weber sensed the atmosphere of urgency as... "we loaded up troops for guard duty on bridges, beaches and defence plants in Virginia, Maryland, Delaware and Pennsylvania. Some of our men and their trucks stayed with these troops."

Berger Bankston was... "despatched with the 116th Infantry aboard our trucks to Camp Pendleton, Virginia to patrol the beaches. They thought the Germans were going to invade the United States that early in the war for some reason. Why they should think Hitler was able to do that at that point I don't know, but we would drive along the beach with the troops on board the truck looking for any invaders who might be coming along the beach."

That winter of 1941/42 was remembered by Glen McIlwee not only for its frantic activity and freezing weather but also for a... "severe bout of Yellow Fever when many men were very ill."

The 29th Division had reached a historic crossroads in their illustrious history and Company 'A' of the 104th Quartermaster Regiment now bade them farewell forever to go their separate way and fight their own war.

Berger Bankston believes... "It was decided after the "Blitzkrieg" was working so well for the Germans that the 29th Division, having 20,000 men, was quite a clumsy division and should be made more mobile and equipped in such a way to make it a faster moving unit. They therefore streamlined the division to 15,000 men, this meant that the 104th Quartermaster Regiment which consisted of three battalions was cut down and called the 29th QM Company."

Chris Controwinski formed a similar opinion... "U.S. Infantry divisions which were known as 'square' divisions, four platoons to a company, four companies to a battalion, four battalions to a regiment were converted to 'triangular' divisions - three platoons to a company, three companies to a battalion etc. As a result of this 'triangularisation' Company 'A' was redesignated 146th QM Truck Company, in effect divorced from the 29th Division. I believe Company 'B' was pulled out at the same time and redesignated the 147th QM Truck Company - and we were individual truck companies."

They were both quite right - it was recognised by the War Department that the old "Square" configuration was ideally suited to mounting frontal attacks on prepared enemy positions as in trench warfare of the First World War, but what they were up against this time was quite different and required some drastic re-thinking.

So in February 1942 the 29th Infantry Division were instructed to convert to a "Triangular" design which took place on March 12th 1942 resulting in the elimination of or transference of some units, the reduction of existing infantry and artillery regiments as well as the contraction of support units which, coupled with the increased number of vehicles allocated would transform the 29th into a flexible and highly mobile fighting unit.

General Order Number 13 had been issued the day before and according to that document the 104th QM Regiment was to be dismembered as follows :-

Hq & Hq Company	-	Redesignated Hq & Hq Co, 104th QM Battalion (less service Platoon).
Service Company	-	Redesignated Service Platoon, Hq Company 104th QM Bn.
Medical Det	-	Redesignated Medical Detachment 104th QM Bn.
Hq 1st Bn	-	Disbanded.
Company A	-	Redesignated Company A, 104th QM Bn (less 2nd Platoon).
Company B	-	Redesignated 2nd Platoon, Company A, 104th QM Bn.
Hq 2nd Bn	-	Disbanded.
Company C	-	Redesignated 146th QM Company (Trk) and reassigned to GHQ.
Company D	-	Redesignated 147th QM Company (Trk) and reassigned to GHQ.
Hq 3rd Bn	-	Disbanded.
Company E	-	Disbanded.
Company F	-	Disbanded.

Rudy Weber accurately recalls this re-shuffle of the 104th QM Regiment which... "was composed of Headquarters Company, Service Company, four Truck Companies - 'A'; 'B'; 'C' and 'D', 'E' Company was Ordnance and 'F' Company with jeeps, command cars and staff cars provided transportation for Divisional Headquarters. All the Division's Ordnance companies - including "E" Company were taken from the QM Regiments and formed the Ordnance branch. "F" Company went to Division Headquarters where they belonged. Service and Headquarters companies were combined. Two of the four Truck Companies were retained to make the 29th Quartermaster Company, and the remaining two Trucking Companies became the 146th and 147th QM Truck Companies. Both of them stayed at Fort Meade as independent outfits and we received all our orders directly from Washington D.C."

But for some reason things didn't work out exactly as General Order 13 intended for although Company 'C' and Company 'D' took up their redesignation on paper as independent Truck Companies, Company 'A' provided all the manpower, vehicles and equipment for the 146th QM Truck Company and Company 'B' likewise for the 147th QM Truck Company, in effect perpetuating their lineage.

Captain James Lyle

A few men were transferred to the 146th from those units that were to be redesignated or disbanded. John Axselle, Walter Duncan and Willie Wilkinson came from Company 'C'; Bob Perry from Company 'D'; George Miley came from Company 'B'; Stuart Oliver and Captain Lyle from Company 'F'.

As a consequence of this re-organisation personnel changes were also made - some came, some went and some stayed. It was a confusing period and Berger Bankston's recollection is that... "Captain Cockrell was transferred to a desk job at headquarters and his place was taken by Captain Lyle who had been in 'F' Company. Lieutenant Beasley from 'C' Company came into the 146th. We had a Lieutenant Sandoz and a Lieutenant Brought. Lieutenant Geoff Miley who commanded the cadre during training of the drafted men later went to the 45th Infantry Division and mustered out as a full Colonel. Our First Sergeant McLemore was over age so he was discharged, and a regular Army First Sergeant from Governors Island, New York, was assigned - his name was Sam McClelland. Other NCOs who were retained from 'A' Company were Staff Sergeant Louis Brienza of the 1st Platoon, Staff Sergeant Reggie Russell of the 2nd Platoon and Staff Sergeant Lester Cox of the 3rd Platoon."

Fred Cox recalls some additions of personnel... "About this time I believe Elroy Toppel came to the 146th from 'F' Company, we also got Lieutenant Albright, he was a newly commissioned Second Lieutenant fresh out of Officers Candidates School which was a three month course - used to call em '90 day wonders'!"

The indiscriminate military administration was now bringing together men of all classes and backgrounds, occasionally taking advantage of an individual's experience or ability however tenuous the connection between their past and anticipated future military use, like Bill Albright... "I had been a school teacher of commercial subjects and a clerk with the Pennsylvania Railroad prior to induction, and I think the reason I was assigned to the 146th was because I had worked at a service station with a petroleum distributor during three of my four years of college and was involved in providing first echelon maintenance."

Bill discovered that... "Captain Lyle had been a Line Foreman with the Virginia Electric Power Company prior to his active service - a leadership type, used to being in charge. Lieutenant Beasley had been a bank teller in Richmond, Virginia - an administrator

Lester Cox

handling payroll and related responsibilities. Lieutenant Brought had been a Regular Army Enlisted Man at Fort Holabird, and his experience in Army Ordnance at the Aberdeen Proving Ground gave him an excellent background for the role of Motor Officer."

The rank structure was also due for a change, and Fred Cox was one who temporarily benefitted... "we got these new stripes, 'Technician' stripes. Our stripes were pointed up and had a black semi-circle, and on that semi-circle there would be a "T", which is actually a Technician 5th Grade. If you had three stripes and a "T" you was a Technician 4th Grade. I was a "T - 5" and as a Technician Cook I got Corporal's pay and didn't have all the hassle like a line corporal would have so it was a good deal. But then later on they was given to all the drivers, so then it wasn't that big a deal money-wise to me. But I kept on being a cook 'cause you worked from noon to noon and you was off from that noon to the following noon and I could come home to Oxon Hill and go back next day and still be there in time to start my shift."

New shoulder patches were issued too, Glenn McIlwee remembers the 146th wearing... "round shoulder patches containing three bars. Red, white and blue denoting Special Service Troops."

Fred Cox sums up the formation and way of life of the new Truck Company... "we changed from 'A' Company 104 QM Regiment, 29th Division to the 146th QM Truck Company, what we call a 'bastard' company, you didn't belong to a division or anything. One time you'd be attached to one outfit for maybe a coupla weeks or month and then it was just a matter of typing up another paper and you'd be transferred to some place else."

Eugene Phillips & Dan Sillers

Changes high in the levels of command had taken place too. In 1941 while still designated as the 104th QM Regiment the 146th QM Truck Company had been part of the Quartermaster Corps under overall though indirect control of the Quartermaster General.

In March 1942 after strenuous resistance from the Quartermaster General - Major General Edmund B. Gregory - the Corps became subordinate to the newly created Services of Supply within days of the alteration being announced.

This had little effect upon the men who drove the trucks but removed them from a cumbersome department of the Corps that encompassed a diverse range of responsibilities to a new, more manageable and specialised controlling branch of the Quartermaster Corps which now re-organised itself into eight general branches, most with a technical specialisation, but all of them subject to the same field conditions as the rest of the Army and organised along military lines.

QUARTERMASTER CORPS (1942)
(re-organised branches)

1. Divisional or Organic

QM company, infantry division
QM company, airborne division
QM pack company, mountain division
Supply battalion, armoured division
QM squadron, cavalry division

2. Administrative

Hq & Hq detachment, QM group
Hq & Hq detachment, QM battalion
Hq & Hq detachment, QM battalion, mobile
Hq & Hq detachment, QM base depot

3. Supply

QM base depot company
QM depot company, supply
QM base depot supply & sales company
QM bakers company
QM railhead company
QM refrigeration company, fixed
QM sales company, mobile
QM remount troop
QM platoon, air depot group (aviation)
QM company, ammunition service group (aviation)
QM company, service group (aviation)
QM depot subsistence company (aviation)

4. Transportation

QM truck company
QM truck company, heavy
QM troop transport company
QM car company
QM refrigeration company, mobile
QM troop, pack
QM truck company (aviation)
QM truck platoon, aviation (separate)

5. Petroleum

QM truck company, petroleum
QM base petroleum supply company
QM gasoline supply company
QM petroleum products laboratory
QM depot company, class III (aviation)

6. Repair and maintenance

QM laundry company, semi mobile
QM salvage repair company, fixed
QM salvage repair company, semi mobile

7. General service and miscellaneous

QM service company
QM graves registration company
QM salvage collecting company
QM fumigation and bath company

8. Composite

CHAPTER SIX

Indiantown Gap Military Reservation, Pennsylvania

28 April - 8 June 1942

8th May 1942:

While Japanese land forces continue to gain ground on all fronts, their advance across the Pacific is checked for the very first time by the "Battle of the Coral Sea" which, although costly in U.S. capital ships, shakes Japanese confidence and forces them to abandon their attack on Port Moresby. This is followed a month later by another U.S. Naval victory in the "Battle of Midway" when four Japanese aircraft carriers are destroyed.

15th May 1942:

Gasoline rationing begins in seventeen states, the weekly ration being three gallons for non-essential vehicles.

28th May 1942:

Rommel's armoured units are in trouble. Having achieved a succession of crushing defeats upon the Allied armies at lightning speed they have outrun their supply lines and are forced to halt through lack of fuel.

30th May 1942:

Britain manages to mount her first thousand bomber raid on Germany boosting the sagging morale of her civilian population and heralding the Royal Air Force's campaign policy of an all out night bombing offensive.

Apart from the acquisition of a new title there was little appreciable difference yet to the style or pace of life for the newly formed 146th. They continued their duties as before, shaking down new personnel and forging their new identity as they went about the more mundane and routine chores. One such task remembered by Rudy Weber... "was to move a Division out of Fort Meade who had just finished being staged to go overseas. After they left we hauled in supplies for the next Division to be staged."

Chris Controwinski was now back from his course and with... "the 146th left Fort Meade and went up to Indiantown Gap which was the base of the 28th Pennsylvania National Guard Division. Our duty there was to haul troops from Indiantown Gap to a railhead in a little place called Lickdale near Lebanon."

Glenn McIlwee also recalls hauling... "the 28th Division to the railhead but after this assignment duties were few and I believe we were waiting on transport to ship out."

One such assignment was to haul the 37th Division to Lickdale where a pleasant surprise awaited Fred Cox... "I happened to see my first cousin Eugene Cox. He'd been in the Engineers in the 29th Division, and when the division changed from a square division to a triangular division they had to get rid of 8,000 men and that's how come we was kicked out and put in the 146th. He was kicked out the 121st Engineers and put in the 37th Division Engineers. That was the last time I saw him 'til after the war was over. He came back from the Pacific to go to OCS and his hair was starting to turn white, he said 'them islands ain't no place to be'. "As time went by, jobs became less frequent and for Rudy Weber... "it was a tough detail - only because we were out all night, every night. If we got two or three hours sleep we were lucky."

CHAPTER SEVEN

Fort George G. Meade,
Maryland

8th June - 27th August 1942

18th June 1942:

Churchill and Roosevelt meet in the United States and reluctantly agree that the opening of a Second Front is simply not possible this year. But a compromise is reached in the form of a North African invasion - Operation "Gymnast", later codenamed "Torch". Stalin is keen for a Second Front to be opened in Europe as he believes this will ease the German army's pressure on his own forces and Churchill has the uncomfortable task of visiting Moscow to inform Stalin of the situation.

28th June 1942:

Air Force General Brereton arrives in Heliopolis, Egypt from India, bringing with him his Tenth Air Force who have been providing bomber and transport support to the Burma campaign.

His arrival at this time is no coincidence for as British forces retreat from Tobruk to El Alamein, Brereton is to command U.S. Army Forces in the Middle East including the Middle East Air Force who will provide combat aircraft in support of ground forces.

The situation is critical for if Rommel breaks through to the Delta area he could swing north and link up with German forces moving south through the Crimea and the Caucasus. Brereton was therefore faced with two possibilities. That Egypt would fall to Rommel, in which case the MEAF would withdraw to bases in Palestine, Syria and Iraq, but should the British Eight Army reverse the situation and take the offensive, then the MEAF will remain in North Africa to support that action until Rommel's ultimate defeat

1st July 1942:

Despite ever lengthening supply lines Rommel's numerically inferior forces reach the outskirts of El Alamein, having repeatedly inflicted heavy losses on the British who appear incapable of a co-ordinated resistance.

7th August 1942:

General Montgomery is given command of the British Eighth Army in North Africa when Churchill's appointed commander General Gott is killed in an air crash.

Squadrons of Brereton's newly formed U.S. Army Middle East Air Force were now arriving one after another at bases in Palestine - Ramat David, Muqueibila and Saint Jean, losing no time in mounting bombing raids on Rommel's army at Mersa Matruh, Tobruk and Benghazi.

17th August 1942:

Rouen, France is the chosen target for the first all-American bombing raid on Europe.

22nd August 1942:

Brazil declares war on Germany after several of her ships become victims of the U-boat campaign which now concentrates its efforts off the Brazilian coast and on the North Atlantic Allied convoy routes - with continuing success.

Returning to Fort Meade, the whole Company with Chris Controwinski... "straightened up our equipment and clothing, the trucks were shipped out."

Berger Bankston was at the railhead at Odenton, Maryland... "loading the trucks on flatcars to go to the port to be shipped overseas. Lester Cox was talking to Captain Lyle. Well Lester was extremely 'goosey', he was so 'goosey' that if you pointed a finger at him he would jump. If you touched him anywhere below the waistline behind his back he would react rather violently. Well, while he was standing there talking to Captain

Dennis Cheeley, William Le Strange and Dan Sillers

Lyle, Sergeant Goodwin went up behind him and goosed him in the seat of the pants and hollered 'Hit him!' - and Lester did - he hit Captain Lyle square on the chin and knocked him about ten feet onto his bottom. Captain Lyle of course knew what the problem was, that Lester would not have done it purposely. I don't think he punished Lester for it but he did issue an order that there would be no more goosing in the 146th!"

Once the trucks were gone Rudy Weber found that... "with not much to do except drill and go to the obstacle course - well, it was just boring."

Fred Cox was bored too, but... "to occupy our time we'd train. Do close order drill, calisthenics and they had this obstacle course, it was supposed to toughen you up or see how tough you were. You shinny over these walls, swing on this rope over a stream of water, crawl across on your belly underneath barbed wire - supposed to separate the men from the boys."

Robert Groce, Robert Perry & Carl Atkins

To maintain discipline during those dreary days of inactivity and waiting a novel method was employed as remembered by Rudy Weber... "Our Company area was on the edge of Fort Meade and just across the road was a wide open boom town. There was no fence, so one hour after reveille the whole Company disappeared. Many a time the Captain and other officers would check the bars in town looking for us but we hid behind the bar. If anyone got caught the standing Company punishment was to dig a six foot by six foot by six foot hole - and then refill it."

This exodus from camp was so widespread that Fred Cox believes Captain Lyle... "decided to do that because if he gave everybody a court martial he wouldn't have anybody but a coupla sergeants and officers in his company, they'd all be in the stockade for being absent without leave!"

Berger Bankston remembers Lester Cox... "got in trouble with Captain Lyle who ordered him to dig a six by six by six hole. Well the temperature was up around the hundred in the summer time and Lester went out on the parade ground and started digging. When he had gone down about four feet Captain Lyle inspected it and said 'Lester that's enough you can quit, fill up the hole'. Lester said 'No sir, you told me to dig it, I'm gonna dig it' and he disobeyed orders and kept on digging, so "Pappy" Lyle said 'OK if that's the way you feel about it, keep on digging'. Lester completed that hole, squared the corners, took every drop of sand out of that hole and made a beautiful six by six by six in that parade ground. Then he filled the hole up, mounded it up like a grave, put a cross on the grave and a note on the cross with his Sergeant's stripes on the top of it saying 'Here lies Sergeant Lester Cox'. He had been busted. Lester would never stay busted very long because he was so valuable as a Sergeant, if he gave a man an order and the man refused to obey it, Lester was man enough to back up his orders."

Bill Albright

There were still occasional chores to be done which helped keep the 146th busy, including Fred Cox... "Every now and again we'd go to Camp Holabird which is a large ordnance base and they would have all this new equipment, cars and trucks, motorcycles, jeeps and trailers, and we'd drive some of those back. They were going to be used by a new division being formed at Fort Meade, the 76th Division in commemoration of 1776, it was called the "Liberty Bell" Division."

Bill Albright had... "joined the 146th in June 1942 after graduating from the Quartermaster School as a member of OCS Class #4, and a month later Lieutenant Broughtk came along as a member of Class #5. He had been a Regular Army Sergeant in the Ordnance, and his arrival filled the Table of Organisation of the 146th for the overseas shipment although we were one officer short. Captain Lyle was the Commanding Officer, Brought was the Motor Officer, Lieutenant Beasley and I were Platoon Leaders, which meant there was a Platoon Leader vacancy that was never filled even when we went overseas. It was the longest preparatory time before actually leaving. We shipped our trucks in July and we'd go home and say 'So long folks, I'm bound overseas' But we don't move, we don't do anything. I get another pass, I go home. It got to be a little embarrassing to be going home on a weekend pass from Fort Meade to western Pennsylvania so many times before we actually left to go to South Carolina."

CHAPTER EIGHT

Charlestown, South Carolina

28th August - 11th September 1942

2nd September 1942:

Rommel's seemingly unstoppable eastward advance has been halted through lack of fuel, his tanks allowing the British forces a brief but important respite to regroup and integrate replacement troops. A turning point in the Axis desert campaign has now been reached with Rommel resolutely refusing to give ground yet unable to advance further for lack of supplies, and the British totally incapable of dislodging him despite mounting reinforcements of men and tanks.

After kicking their heels for so long with no vehicles, no convoys and little else to do, it was with relief that the 146th were placed on a train with Berger Bankston..."and sent to Sullivans Island, South Carolina at which time we thought we were headed for the boat and rumour had us going to Sullivans Island as a ploy to fool any saboteurs who might be trying to find what we were doing."

It was certainly confusing - Chris Controwinski remembers..."It was supposed to be a big secret, not let anybody know, don't write home, don't call home, don't say where you are or what's going on."

Fred Cox was with them as they..."left on a train and went to Charleston, South Carolina to a camp down there. While we were there we were issued new rifles and we had to take them apart and get all the cosmoline off."

According to Rudy Weber they were..."British Lee-Enfields. - a unique case of 'Lend - Lease' in reverse!"

With his new rifle Fred Cox and all the others..."went out to Fort Moultrie Island in Charleston harbour, went over this real high bridge to get to it I remember. We's riding in the back, let somebody else drive. On the ranges you would fire out over the water, so they had to stick up flags to keep the boats from coming too close while we were firing."

Berger Bankston..."stayed there about two weeks during which time we spent a great deal of time on the rifle range shooting up ammunition, we were given boxes of ammunition and told to shoot it up any way we felt like, from any position, just get the feel of our rifle and fall in love with that rifle. We shot so many rounds our shoulders were blue."

Glenn McIlwee was quite surprised about the whole episode..."Upon arrival I expected to ship out, but after a week or two in camp there we entrained back to Fort Dix - I'm guessing our designated ship had been sunk!"

CHAPTER NINE

Fort Dix, New Jersey

12th - 21st September 1942

12th September 1942:

German U-boat 'U-156' making its way to the Cape of Good Hope area attacks and sinks the liner *Laconia* which is carrying Allied servicemen's wives and children as well as Italian prisoners-of-war. The U-boat commander surfaces to help the survivors and radios the Allied authorities for assistance, but is attacked by an American plane. This reaction prompts Admiral Doenitz to order his U-boats never again to make similar rescue attempts.

The 146th now embarked upon their great adventure. It was a very subdued affair, there was no fanfare or flag-waving, in fact there was very little to mark the occasion and many may have missed the significance of their departure from South Carolina. It began simply enough with a train ride, but as Fred Cox recalls..."It was an old coal burning locomotive and that soft coal dust and smoke coming back through the windows that were open 'cause it was hot, our clothes got black, coal dust got on our faces like some of your Negro troops. That was like three or four o'clock in the afternoon, we rode pretty much all night up to New Jersey."

Berger Bankston also remembers the train journey that..."was supposed to be a secret movement, however as we went through some of the towns along the way, factory workers were hanging out of the factory windows waving at us and cheering us. They knew it was a troop train I guess and I think we broke some regulations by raising the blinds and waving back. We went to Fort Dix, New Jersey where we stayed just a few days."

Before going overseas Captain Lyle..."assembled the Company and told us, 'We're going overseas, we have two hundred dollars in the Company fund which we haven't spent and with your permission I have something to spend it on' and of course the Company gave him permission to do so. He purchased enough Zippo lighters - the type you could put on a string and lower in the gas tank of your truck and fill it with gasoline, which we did the whole time we were in Africa - for each man in the Company to have two, everyone was issued one and a second was kept in reserve in case you lost it. He also purchased a large supply of condoms to make sure that the men would be protected from disease, overseas knowing men and what they would be doing. The rest of the money was used to buy three shortwave radios, one for each platoon so they would have at least one radio where we could keep up with news. That was money well spent."

On Glenn McIlwee's 28th birthday, the 20th of September 1942, he and his colleagues..."were transported to New York harbor, and by way of the Staten Island ferry boarded the steamship *Aquitania*."

Fred Cox's recollection of embarkation was that..."We waited for the ship to get loaded, so Sunday afternoon we hiked about a mile with full packs to the train, got on the train and rode for several hours, got on a ferry boat and rode that for several hours. I know it got cold on the water, we didn't have no place to sit, we just sat on the deck until it tied up to a big warehouse. We walked through the warehouse and kept walking, next thing I know I was on a ship! I never did see the side of the ship, but all of a sudden I realised I was inside it. The gangway was almost like a tunnel, it was completely covered over. We got on at "E" deck and we were quartered on "G" deck. "F" and "G" decks were below the water line, and about forty of us were in a room no more than about thirty foot square."

The *Aquitania* left New York harbour as Berger Bankston recalls..."at 6 o'clock in the morning with two destroyers, a blimp and a PBY overhead for protection, travelling at 26 knots - which was full speed - on a zigzag course for Rio de Janeiro."

Below decks Fred Cox was perplexed..."on each bunk was two little pillows hooked together with a cloth strap - I didn't know what they were for a little while 'til I found out they were life preservers! Supposed to put one pillow in front of you and one behind you then you pulled the cloth tapes around and tied in a bow on your chest."

So the 146th Quartermaster Truck Company of four Officers and one hundred and nine Enlisted Men left the land that many would not see for over a thousand days.

CHAPTER TEN

At sea - s.s. *Aquitania*

21st September - 31st October 1942

2nd October 1942:

The Royal Navy cruiser H.M.S. *Curacao* is accidentally rammed and sunk by the *Queen Mary* while they are both manoeuvring in the Western Approaches with the loss of many of the *Curacao's* crew. Passengers lining the rail of the *Queen Mary* who witness this tragedy are men of the 29th Infantry Division on their way to Greenock, Scotland.

23rd October 1942:

General Montgomery's arrival in the desert coincided with the advent of fresh reinforcements and equipment which helped him to achieve at the battle of El Alamein everything that had been dreamed of and striven for by his many predecessors. Just before midnight his offensive at El Alamein opened against two groups of Axis forces separated by lack of fuel - and despite elaborate preparations and training for this thrust with an almost two to one superiority in men and equipment, Montgomery's troops fail to keep to the battle timetable. To the fury of Churchill the battle grinds to a halt while Montgomery regroups his forces under continual counter-attacks and is forced to alter the direction of his main thrust westward. Rommel is unable to withstand such pressure, his options severely restricted by a lack of fuel, ammunition and supplies and he is inexorably forced back, fighting every inch of the way.

Considerable support had come from the U.S. Middle East Air Force, who, over the fourteen days of battle had flown 1366 sorties dropping thousands of tons of bombs on Axis shipping and road convoys, Fighters had not only downed 45 enemy aircraft but another 55 were probably destroyed. They had attacked targets of opportunity and the desert was littered with burnt-out tanks and vehicles, opening the way for the Eighth Army.

The *Aquitania* in 1942 was an ageing thoroughbred. Built on the River Clyde in Scotland in 1913 as a trans-Atlantic liner she had been requisitioned by the British Admiralty early in the First World War and converted into an armed merchant cruiser but was found to be too big. She was paid off and returned to her owners only to be requisitioned again, used first as a military transport vessel and later as a hospital ship until 1918 when she fulfilled her final military role of that conflict repatriating American and Canadian troops. She returned to take up her original civilian role as a mail ship and luxury liner carrying over 3,000 passengers on each trip, and by 1925 had completed her one hundredth trans - Atlantic round voyage.

But by 1942 she was again in military service, sailing her familiar Atlantic route, this time running the gauntlet of German submarine "wolf packs" which, by October 1942 had sunk 637,000 precious tons of Allied shipping.

Rommel's "Afrika Korps" have become a casualty of their own success by stretching supply lines too far, easily romping after the retreating British forces and panicking them to such an extent that they are on the point of implementing evacuation plans to withdraw from Egypt and regroup in Eritrea.

The 146th were to be part of this regrouping scheme and as far as Chris Controwinski knew..."We were supposed to be going to Asmara in Eritrea because when we left the States, Rommel was still banging on the gates of Alexandria, but we didn't know what the hell was going on. We were supposed to go to Asmara to supply the British and American air force people until such time as we were needed in Egypt."

Bill Albright had a little more detail..."When we received our orders at sea aboard the *Aquitania* the battle of El Alamein had not been fought, and the (U.S.) Service of Supply headquarters in Cairo was scheduled to fall back to Eritrea. The 146th' mission there would be to operate trucks from the port of Massawa at sea level up the mountainside to 6,000 feet above sea level to the city of Asmara. At that time it was our understanding that the American forces were preparing to evacuate Cairo and fall back to a position in Ethiopia as the headquarters as the Service of Supply in the Middle East."

American military interests in the Middle East had been present since 1941 and were originally divided in half by convenient geographic boundaries. Simply entitled the 'North African Mission' and the 'Iranian Mission' they were retitled in June 1942 when the Middle East was designated as a theatre of operations and given the title of 'United States Army Forces in the Middle East' - (USAFIME).

USAFIME retained the same two geographic areas which were then renamed the 'North African Service Command' - responsible for operations in Egypt and Palestine, and the 'Iran-Iraq Service Command' for operations in the Persian Gulf.

Under the command of Major General R. L. Maxwell of the Service of Supply, USAFIME took control of the newly formed U.S. Army Middle East Air Force which was commanded by Major General Lewis H. Brereton.

At the very hour of this rationalisation, the Afrika Korps smashed through British lines in Libya and drove almost unimpeded to within seventy miles of Alexandria. Within days all U.S. Army projects in Egypt and Palestine were halted, personnel moved to Eritrea along with the headquarters of the North African Service Command and USAFIME began burning files in preparation for leaving Egypt.

But the British held Rommel at El Alamein, and by August USAFIME activities were resumed in Palestine and Cairo, Egypt under a simplified command structure. The North African Service Command was gone and replaced by three smaller service commands that had originally been under its jurisdiction.

The Heliopolis Area became Delta Service Command covering all of Egypt, the Palestine Area - Levant Service Command, and territories to the south became the Eritrea Service Command.

With so few opportunities at this stage of hostilities for U.S. ground troops to confront European Axis forces, the mission of both the Middle East and European Theatres was to conduct an aerial warfare campaign.

Oblivious to the surging tides of the desert conflict most of the men aboard the *Aquitania*, including Berger Bankston had more immediate and fundamental matters to attend to..."When we left New York harbour the first morning we ran into extremely rough seas and with 7,000 men on board I expect all 7,000 of them were seasick. Men were fifteen deep at the rail scrambling, trying to get to the rail to lean overboard to be sick - well they didn't make it. The decks and the corridors of that ship were two inches thick with vomit. The toilets were running over with it, the vanity washbowls were running over with it, and that ship had such a foul odour to it for the rest of the voyage it was unbelievable. You had the feeling that you didn't want to use the vanity as a washbowl to wash your face after seeing what had been in it."

Some were luckier, like Glen McIlwee who..."never once suffered from this affliction" and was able to notice that..."one of the ship's screws was out of balance. The ship listed on every zig and back on every zag and when the prop on the out of balance screw came near the surface, there was a noticeable vibration - the entire ship shuddered."

The weather and sea conditions did not improve. On Tuesday the 22nd September Bill McMaster awoke..."and the ship was rolling and groaning so that it felt as if it were going to snap. Down in the chow line in the mess hall, where the rolling motion was at its worst, men would get sick and not being able to get through the mob to the door, would slip off to the nearest corner where they would crouch and deposit the contents of their stomachs."

Chris Controwinski didn't think much of the food either..."We got lousy British chow, we hated their damned mutton, we didn't think it was fit to eat. We weren't used to it but, oh God! It wasn't prepared very well and it looked like slop to us. We used to bang our mess kits when it was chow time, we'd get in line and rattle our mess kits and go "Baaaa" and we'd drive the cooks crazy but I don't think we'd have survived on that mutton. Thank God they had a Post Exchange Commissary on board ship. If you stood in line long enough and had enough money you could buy cakes and candy and assorted goodies that in effect kept us from starving to death."

Berger Bankston stood in the chow line one day..."and the meat in the stew was green-looking, so we had a near riot on board and they called for the Colonel in command of the troops to come down and look at the meat and Lester Cox put a piece of it up under his nose and asked him if he would eat it, and he said "No" he would not. The food improved considerably after that."

The sea conditions also improved, the weather grew hotter and Bill McMaster found another exasperation..."Drinking fountains are only turned on for short intervals during the day, and now a ruling has come out forbidding anyone to take along his canteen and fill it. The men wait in long lines for a drink, and frequently the water is shut off before they get to it. I have been taking care of the problem for myself by drinking at each meal as much as possible of the muddy coloured liquid put on the tables. No-one has yet figured out whether it is supposed to be coffee or British tea, actually I think it is sometimes one and sometimes the other. Anyway the boys don't go in much for drinking the stuff, it tastes like dirty, warm dish water."

Then things got worse again as Bill describes..."To make life really miserable, we have been informed that everything in our cabins (we're nineteen in ours) must be uniform. This is next to impossible since every square inch of space is needed, and we can get along only by jamming barracks bags, etc., wherever we can find a particle of space. Every day it's the same old story. Take that barracks bag out of that corner nook; there's not a similar nook for every bag and it spoils the uniformity of the room. Pile them in the bathroom if necessary. Better take that pack down from there; ask the fellow over there if he would mind if it's hung from the cot above him. It'll inconvenience him a little but it will make things uniform that way."

With considerable relief they made their first landfall - the Brazilian port of Rio de Janeiro - on Saturday 3rd of October and Berger Bankston recalls spending..."three days in the harbour taking on oil, water and food at which time the troops were quite fascinated with Christ' Statue on top of the mountain, the girls on the ferry boats and a Brazilian battleship in the harbour which we determined was one of our old ones we had given to Brazil. "

After three days of replenishment and no shore leave, Berger Bankston and the Aquitania..."proceeded to cross the Atlantic alone after our two destroyer escort out of Rio left us, they couldn't go the same speed we went as we were wide open."

Time really dragged as Glen McIlwee found..."nothing happened on board. Some men gambled all the time. I tried to read a book each day - trucks had dumped (literally) books on board ship before sailing. Some did nothing, some cleaned rifles all the time - or so it seemed - because of the salty air. I was on 'G' deck, two decks below the water line right above the engine room, so it was nice and dry and hot - no need to clean rifles the entire voyage!"

As the *Aquitania* approached South African waters Bill McMaster heard a report..."over the radio that an Allied ship was torpedoed and sunk off the coast of Capetown a couple of days ago. We have been wearing overcoats with cartridge belt and canteen since then, on the alert for a possible sinking at any time." On Monday the 12th of October..."About ten minutes ago two cruisers came in sight to escort us into Capetown. They're out ahead of us now. We expect to hit Capetown tomorrow."

But before they did Berger Bankston recalls..."we encountered submarines and began circling. The troops realised this and began spreading all kinds of rumours. The ship suddenly heeled over to almost ninety degrees on its side, and standing on the stern of the ship I watched a torpedo miss us by about fifteen or twenty feet."

Garland Coghill later discovered that..."Nazi propaganda had us sunk quite a few times we were out there."

So real was the threat of enemy submarines that Glen McIlwee saw..."the bay at Capetown was chained and submarine nets were up. These were opened and the ship drove in - fast! When the tug boats pushed the *Aquitania* against the pier, all the lifeboats on that side of the ship were crushed - and were never replaced."

After docking everyone including Berger Bankston..." dearly wanted to go ashore, so we were told to clean up our uniforms but no-one would be allowed ashore unless they shaved. Many of us had tried to grow beards having decided not to shave until we got to where we were going and we had something like 23 days growth of beard which had to be shaved off if you wanted to go ashore - with cold salt sea water! You can imagine what a horrible shave that was and how many nicks we had on our faces, but we shaved and we went ashore."

Chris Controwinski went ashore..."with the equivalent of five dollars and headed for the first restaurant we could find where we could get a steak, and we blew most of our money on that. People were very kind, they latched onto us, took us sightseeing, took us to their homes, bought meals for those of us who'd blown their money on beer. We sorta went wild."

Bill McMaster..."Found Capetown surprisingly Americanized."

But it was only surface deep as Berger Bankston discovered..."a milk shake sign - 'American Milk Shakes' - we ordered one and when it was prepared it was nothing like an American milk shake but was just goats milk with a little flavouring in it which I couldn't drink." There were other similarities..."They had a sign that said 'Europeans only' we didn't understand what that was all about but later found out that was the counterpart to our signs in the United States which said 'Whites only'."

Fred Cox was..."allowed one afternoon ashore, being cautioned not to tell anyone what ship we were on as some of the people of South Africa were sympathetic to the Germans. My three buddies and I met this civilian and he seemed to know more than we did so we tried to be as non-committal as possible to his questions, separated from him and went sightseeing."

Reluctantly Berger Bankston and all the others..."got back to the ship and were told that the next morning at nine o'clock we would parade in the city. No American troops had ever been there before and we would put on a parade for the people of Capetown. So we pressed our khaki uniforms, we shined our brass, we shined our shoes and we got ready for that parade at nine o'clock, however at six o'clock the ship left port. We understood later that parade was a ploy to fool any saboteurs who might have been in Capetown as to when we were leaving the port so they might tip off a submarine. Although we were disappointed not to go ashore again, we understood."

Just before leaving Capetown the *Aquitania* had taken on about two thousand men of the Royal South African Air Force to the delight of Glen McIlwee..."all these lovely chaps must have been song and dance fellows, for every hour of the twenty four in a day for the rest of the voyage, the piano and numerous musical instruments were played constantly - and so much singing! A rare change of pace thanks to them - and what talent!"

Four days out of Capetown, Bill McMaster records..."Today a man of the crew broke the monotony for us a bit by falling overboard. Fortunately the water was not as rough as it has been, and when the ship circled around we found him still swimming on top, about a half hour after he had fallen in."

Berger Bankston recalls there was some concern about this man as he had been taken on as a crew member in Capetown and was subsequently found to have Nazi sympathies, which gave rise to the speculation that he had perhaps signalled to a waiting U-Boat and then dived overboard to save himself before the *Aquitania* was torpedoed by the submarine.

Fred Cox was amused by Allen Nichols..."only a couple more days before we's getting off the ship, he sneaked up to 'C' deck where the officers were. They had bathtubs and all up there 'cause this was a pleasure ship. He goes up there with a towel around him and goes in the bathroom - 'cause you don't have bars of rank on the towel and he was only in his thirties so he looked as if he could have been an officer. So he goes in and runs the water in the bathtub, takes his bath and then thinks he's gonna wash his life preserver a little bit, so he throws it in the water and sits on it and the darn thing sinks! Sinks to the bottom of the tub! He said 'All the time I bin thinking that daggone things gonna support me in the water and here it won't even hold my weight and I ain't got no clothes on!"

Bill McMaster remarked..."Things are beginning to look interesting ahead for us when we get to Egypt. We have been listening to lectures daily on the people and about their money system, their language etcetera. From what we are told things must be very strange in Egypt. One thing I have noticed on the "Ship's News" is repeated air attacks on Cairo. It seems we will be located at a little town a short way from Cairo called something like "Heliopolis". It would seem that we will see enough bombing - I don't exactly like that."

Bill Albright was responsible for some of these lectures as..."the schoolteacher in me decided that we should draw an outline map of the countries in the Middle East and part of the training that I did during the voyage was to try to teach some Middle East geography utilising a mimeographed map showing boundaries but not showing the names of countries."

At last the journey was almost over and the final port of call before arrival in Egypt was at Aden. Bill McMaster noted..."Part of the shoreline is marked by jagged peaks and at other points the shore seems to give way to vast level stretches of sand. This is the most barren country I've ever seen in my life. Not a tree is in sight anywhere, nor a blade of grass to be seen."

As the unhappy experience of the *Aquitania* drew to a close, it is summed up by Berger Bankston's poem.

"AQUITANIA"

So this is a troopship the scourge of the earth
a sailors heaven a soldiers hell from the time she leaves her berth
the food is infected with bugs maggots and rot
to a Yankee soldier its just plain slop
you sleep in a hammock that devilish invention
while officers and nurses with dishonourable intention
sleep in cabins and state rooms the best to be had

they know no discomfort only luxury begad
we arrive in a port of worldly renown
with a terrible craving to go into town
but we must stay on this rotten old ship
salute all the officers and take all their ----
God grant us safe passage to the USA
and then God willing we'll have our day
with freedom justice and peace evermore
with no more troopships and no more war.

At Tewfik, on the Suez isthmus Berger Bankston disembarked on..."little sailboats with motors on them, came out to the ship to take us ashore, and we were disembarking after dark. They'd put ten or twenty of us on the little boat and shuttled us ashore and go back and get more. They put us in tents when we got ashore and told us to get some sleep."

It was miraculous that any arrangements for their arrival were made at all for it was the responsibility of the U.S. Army Transportation Corps who had only just arrived in the Middle East themselves, hurriedly forming their organisation from the Transportation Section of the Quartermaster Corps.

Their task was made easier as once they learned details of passengers and cargo expected, and knew their destination, this was passed to the British who did all the work. They made out movement orders, arranged berthing and unloading of vessels and saw to transportation by either rail, truck or ship to the stated final destination.

Those first steps on Egyptian soil are remembered by a careful Chris Controwinski..."it was Halloween night, October 31st 1942. They had given us these lectures all the time those forty days and nights we were on board ship - whatever you do if you drop anything on the ground for God's sake leave it lay because the place is filthy, there's nothing but disease etcetera, adinfinitum. They had tents set up with ditches that you dove into in case of an air raid, and some used them as latrines - thank God there was no air raid!"

Glen McIlwee remembers those lectures too..."about the filth. We were cautioned to make as little contact with the ground as possible, so after sleeping on the sand for several nights, we were transported to Cairo."

Bill McMaster's welcome to Egypt was by a few squatting natives..."with a greeting we were soon to become accustomed to - "Cigarette? - Give cigarette?" The following morning..."after a good breakfast cooked by a Scottish Mess Corporal and a bunch of Egyptian KP's for the first time since we had crossed the Atlantic we saw a few trees of some kind off in the distance. At about five in the afternoon we loaded our barracks bags on a truck, got back into our harnesses, took up our rifles, and marched to a railroad station where we boarded a crude Egyptian train and set off towards Cairo. Everywhere the train stopped the brown-skins would line the track trying to bum cigarettes. Some carried trinkets, which they tried to sell for either piastres or cigarettes. If you gave one a cigarette he put it inside his clothes and hit the next soldier for another one."

The s.s. *Aquitania* continued as a troop transport for the remainder of the War and in 1945 sailed her last patriotic voyage carrying 1,200 wounded American soldiers from Glasgow to New York. She ended her days back in Scotland - finally broken up for scrap in 1950.

CHAPTER ELEVEN

Camp Russell B. Huckstep, Egypt

Ever since 1940 when the Italian army had arrogantly strutted across their Libyan border into Egypt, conventional battle lines between British and Axis forces had flowed back and forth countless times across the same strip of desert. From the Mediterranean cost it stretched inland only a few miles, included the only hardtop road running from east to west and concentrated the might and efforts of opposing armies locked in a seemingly unbreakable stalemate.

Various remedies were applied by the frustrated British and Empire forces who were quite unable to achieve that one decisive victory to tip the balance in their favour. In desperation they changed the titles of their armies and regularly replaced commanders at all levels to no avail until General Bernard Law Montgomery assumed command by default, and miraculously breathed new life into a tired and dispirited Eighth Army.

Montgomery's desert army was spiced with a few American tank crews who had established themselves at Heliopolis, also known as Darb el Hagg, Camp Kilo 19, and eventually - Camp Russell B. Huckstep.

In addition to the American tank crews the U.S. Army Air Force were also represented in the Western desert, by squadrons flying with the Royal Air Force since September 1941 under the collective title of the "Middle East Air Force".

These American elements of the "MEAF" had been commanded by General Lewis H. Brereton since his arrival in North Africa in June 1942, and as the American presence was scheduled to increase in this theatre it was thought prudent to place their operations on an independent footing.

This commenced on 18th November 1942 when authority was given to activate the U.S. Ninth Air Force commanded by General Brereton and formed from existing American units already flying with the "MSAF".

Their immediate task was to provide air transport of gasoline for the advancing Eighth Army at the rate of 190 tons per day and achieved this by borrowing fifty-two C-47s from the 316th Troop Carrier Group of the "Africa Air Transport", hauling gasoline 250 miles to the front in just under two hours.

Their finest achievement in one day was to carry 48,510 gallons forward which would have taken fifty-nine trucks three days to reach the same destination over a 425 mile road route - a comparison of pure hypothesis for at this time there weren't that number of trucks available.

Alongside these supply missions the Ninth Air Force continued their bombing campaigns - Tripoli was attacked by heavy bombers of the 98th and 376th Bomb Groups on 22nd November 1942 with some success, and as noted at the time was the port's first aerial attack since the western offensive began, and the first U.S. action against the city since the early 1800's when American Marines stormed ashore to curb the activities of Tripolitanian pirates.

On 4th December 1942 Liberators of the same two Bomb Groups attacked Naples harbour, reporting hits on several Italian Navy ships marking another milestone for the Ninth Air Force as it was the first U.S. attack on the Italian mainland.

To support their flying operations the Ninth Air Force required an efficient supply and support organisation and by early November 1942 the U.S. Middle East Theatre of Operations had organised the creation of a Service of Supply headquarters to oversee their Service Commands.

"Delta" Service Command was responsible for the Cairo area until 16th February 1944 when there was a title change to the "Middle East" Service Command. The eastern Mediterranean including Palestine was under the jurisdiction of the "Levant" Service Command.

On 7th December 1942 the short lived "Libyan" Service Command was created as the Allied armies pushed westward re-taking the majority of Libya from the Axis. This command being responsible for the Tripoli and Cyrenaica sub-areas until 26th May 1943.

According to plan more and more units arrived to swell the ranks of the U.S. Air Force in the Western Desert, coming under the control of USAFIME. General Brereton being appointed Commander on 31st January 1943.

By now the American tankmen had moved west with the Eighth Army bequeathing Camp Kilo 19 to the 146th - their first real home in North Africa before the three platoons were dispersed across 1,500 miles of the Middle East.

Berger Bankston learned something of the brief history of Huckstep..."which was a very hastily constructed camp that had been put together for the American tank troops sent there ahead of us. They were the first Americans to arrive in that area approximately three months before we did and their purpose was to train the British Eighth Army how to drive, handle and maintain the General Grant tanks which they were using at that time, and also for the Americans to get some battle experience. Learning something about desert and tank warfare those men actually took part in the battles fought by the British Eighth Army. Later on we saw some motion pictures in which they were portrayed, I think Humphrey Bogart starred in one of them and we probably learned more about them from watching the movie than we did when we were there."

But it was the USAFIME Service Commands that the 146th were destined to serve principally, the 9th Air Force in particular, and almost straight away things started happening.

John Axselle arrived..."at Huckstep and we couldn't have been there over a week and they wanted a platoon to go to Palestine where they were going to establish this big depot up there. The Germans were coming through southern Russia and the military strategists felt they were gonna come down through Palestine and into Egypt in a big pincer."

Bill Albright remembers it was..."The 3rd Platoon of the 146th that departed Camp Kilo 19 for Palestine. Initially to provide transport for civilian contractors who were building an Ordnance depot in Tel-a-Viv in anticipation of a German thrust southward from the Balkans towards Cairo. Officers of the 146th began a series of rapid changes, replacements and re-assignments from the very moment they arrived.

INITIAL ROSTER

146th QM Co. (Trk)   November 30 1842

Signed: Clifford M Beasley
1st Lt

0-346479	Captain LYLE, James C	QMC NG	11-8-41 Commanding Officer Duty
0-387310	1st Lt BEASLEY, Clifford M	QMC Ng	27-1-42 Platoon Commander Duty
0-1573003	2nd Lt ALBRIGHT, William R	QMC AUS	23-5-42 Platoon Commander Duty
0-1575791	2nd Lt BROUGHT, Calvin R	AUS	15-7-42 Platoon Commander D S

Remembering that the 146th were already one officer under-strength Bill Albright found himself in a unique position and describes how it came about..."Captain Lyle upon arriving in Egypt was transferred to the Quartermaster Depot and later promoted to Major, so that meant we were one more officer short. Lieutenant Brought assumed the position of 3rd Platoon Leader and went to Palestine. That meant there was only myself left to go out on the convoys. Cliff Beasley was made acting Commanding Officer of the 146th and later promoted to Captain. He did the Morning Reports, administration and supply - Commanding Officers never went on convoys, they always stayed back at the headquarters doing paperwork. I was promoted to First Lieutenant effective 1st January 1943 and started the convoy activity. Actually I was the only Platoon Leader assigned to the Company that was operating in Egypt so consequently I took all the early convoys."

In camp the 146th were being initiated into desert customs and culture which was a novel process that surprised Berger Bankston..."we took our meals

Capt Beasley, Lt Brought & Lt Sinclair

in the mess hall and one of the things that sort of shocked us immediately - the cook had a huge black snake whip. And when the Arabs would try to steal garbage out of the garbage cans he would go outside with the black snake whip and beat them away. I couldn't understand why he didn't let them go ahead and eat the garbage. He could talk Arabic quite well, he'd been there long enough I guess to learn some of the language. I later found that there not only was a problem with the Arabs trying to take leftovers out of your mess kit when you came out the door, scrambling and begging and fighting each other for it, but they also had a bird called a Kitehawk which we understood had been imported, because Egypt did not have buzzards to eat carrion. Those Kitehawks would dive down and try to take the leftovers out of your mess kit. One of them hit me on the shoulder and almost knocked me down trying to get food out of my mess kit, and I soon learned when you walk out the mess hall door, you throw your mess kit on the floor and let the birds and Arabs fight over it, and when they get through, go pick your mess kit up and wash it out."

The 146th were learning fast - whatever Chris Controwinski learned he believes..."we learned from the British at first. It was a while before our GMC 6x6's came in. Out there they had a lot of broken down Canadian 1½ ton stake trucks and a lot of British equipment that they didn't have parts for so they told us to get to work, make what we could out of it. So we scrounged up as many of these Canadian Fords and jeeps that were non-operational and cannibalised some of 'em and made some of 'em operational - that would be November and December of 1942. We started three and four truck convoys hauling gasoline out on the Western Desert but we didn't go very far."

Berger Bankston also remembers those Fords..."we put together I guess maybe fifteen, twenty or more trucks in good running condition."

One of those early convoys was taken out by Bill Albright..."using some Lend-Lease English Fords whereby some of the members of our convoy got separated and then endeavoured to rejoin us and had the misfortune of causing the deaths of two British motorcyclists. I remember having to write a report concerning this unfortunate incident, and shortly thereafter - I must have written a good report or something - they put me on detached service from the 146th as the Post Motor Pool Officer. On assuming that job I brought with me our then Dispatcher, Glenn McIlwee to assist in fielding the requests for transportation which were channelled through the Post Headquarters."

They were both placed on detached service about the 15th of November 1942 on the Post Commander's staff. The Post Commander was a West Point Lieutenant Colonel named William C. Paunty, his branch was Horse Cavalry and Bill's assessment of him was as..."a good officer".

Those early convoys presented some unexpected hazards for Fred Cox..."Sometimes the British MPs would chase us for speeding too much and we could actually outrun 'em when we had our trucks wide open. We used to do different little tricks on the British Redcaps, we'd tell 'em our name was Abraham Lincoln or George Washington and they'd write that down, and we'd tell 'em we were hauling for the "Balloon Squadron". After a little while they started catching on, they didn't believe nothing - 'You damned Yanks!', still we had a lot of fun to start with anyway."

Battlefields of the Western Desert had so far been a predominantly British theatre of operations, and now things were going in their favour they felt it was only right that the illusion of an all-British campaign should be preserved. That's when Fred Cox..."got these pith helmets from the British, had cork in 'em I think, we had shorts like the British and a shirt - we looked like British troops. We had this little strip of cloth on our shoulder that said "United States", but with the Scots and the Aussies and the Kiwis we all looked alike. Wintertime we had British battle dress, a little short jacket and pants with buttons on to button the jacket to the pants and they had these short canvas leggings so the pants'd blouse over a little bit. We wore our own overseas caps. They said the reason we had to wear them was to keep all the troops looking alike 'cause with our green fatigue clothing, might think we was Germans and someone might want to shoot at us!

The reason for wearing British uniforms given to Rudy Weber was..." so that any Germans flying over wouldn't know how many Americans we had there, yet our American trucks had a large star painted on both doors and the hood".

Bill Albright..."went to pick up our own trucks and as we were forming up a convoy the Egyptian urchins were climbing on the running boards and talking to the men, and somehow several of our men lost their wristwatches. It seems that a very sharp razor blade cut the wristband and suddenly they were without a wristwatch!"

When their own trucks finally arrived of course they were still U.S. Army olive drab, John Axselle recalls..."we had to paint 'em desert camouflage with a damned sand storm raging."

Fred Cox remembers the..."desert colour, it was almost like an ivory, and we had to put this big white circle with a white star in the centre of it for American identification."

Once reunited with their own trucks, convoy work began in earnest and B e r g e r B a n k s t o n recalls one of t h e i r routines..."We would never go back from the forward areas without taking something with us, usually in the form of empty petrol cans which w o u l d b e refilled and taken back to the front."

Convoy at rest

But the front-line was constantly and rapidly moving - Rommel's Afrika Korps were now retreating so far so fast that they were often beyond the operational range of many of the USAFIME bombers who reverted to training missions, and fighter squadrons had to divide their ground crews into "A" and "B" parties - one to service the aircraft while the other moved ahead to the next landing ground - an arrangement well illustrated when the 57th Fighter Group operated from fifteen airstrips in three months.

As momentum of the Eighth Army's westward advance increased from the battle of Alamein onwards it left Camp Kilo 19 deep in the rear area where the two remaining platoons of the 146th celebrated their desert Christmas of 1942 with Fred Kennel ..."in charge of an Allied Mess Hall twenty four hours a day. I fed Italians, Germans, Foreign Legion, Poles, Yugos, English, Scotch, New Zealanders, Aussies, etcetera. I made many friends and never refused anyone as long as I had supplies. Out in the desert I'd stop camel caravans and trade "Victory" cigarettes for fresh eggs for the troops and we'd deal in Arab markets for fresh produce when possible. Our first Christmas in Egypt one or two of our lads stole an evergreen out of King Farouk's palace grounds and we decorated it with ends of food cans."

Fred was still running a mess hall at Camp Kilo 19 when he befriended a..."51st Highlander who deserted his unit in the desert and remained with us for nearly a month. He had battle fatigue and didn't care what happened to him although he begged us to return him to his unit before a month was up or else he would be shot!"

Fred's time in the mess was a pleasant interlude from his more usual workplace in the back of a kitchen truck where he worked miracles with a petrol burning range, designated the "M-1937" model which comprised of several metal cabinets each with a roast or bake pan with a griddle cover, heated from a fire unit and a boiler.

One morning at camp he woke to find himself quite alone in a deserted and eerily silent camp. Searching around Fred came across the only other occupant, Lieutenant McMaster - now with the 147th - who was equally perplexed as to where the others were. Fred was incensed ..."everyone left camp and left me with all this mess, who the hell is going to clean it up? McMaster asked 'who's left?' and I said "Me and you!' He said "Let's get busy and clean up this -----'. I washed and he dried!" They found our later that the Company had been called out for convoy duty at five minutes notice, every available driver and vehicle had gone and neither knew anything about it.

The mess arrangements since the 146th arrived at Camp Kilo 19 was, as Bill Albright recalls..."that the 146th and 147th kitchen personnel combined to operate the mess hall the first time we were at Huckstep. Afterwards, when the 146th were based at Benghazi and Tripoli, the Huckstep Mess which fed transients etc., continued to function with Truck Company kitchen personnel until Captain Sandoz brought the Headquarters section up to Benghazi, at which time the 404th QM Truck Company and a Special Services unit took over operation of the Huckstep Mess."

Camp Kilo 19 was rapidly becoming one of the largest U.S. Quartermaster depots in the Western Desert with the 110th Ordnance Depot alongside the one thousand bed 38th General Hospital - recognised as the leading hospital in this theatre, established in October 1942 and caring for American air force battle casualties from their forays against the enemy throughout North Africa, Sicily, Tunisia, Greece, Rumania and Italy.

There was always contact with the local population and the Arab way of life was a constant source of amazement to Berger Bankston, particularly when..."we made a convoy down the Sweetwater Canal where we saw people washing clothes in the canal, other people drinking from the canal and buffalo urinating in the canal and this gave us some idea how those people lived. We saw people sitting around a communal bowl in their houses eating and we saw goats and hogs pressing past their shoulders to help themselves out of the same bowl! That kinda turned us off a little."

The city of Cairo was close to Darb el Hagg and Berger Bankston recalls the relative peace and calm of its whitewashed houses and bustling narrow streets spasmodically erupting in violence and death, sometimes coming from the most unexpected quarters..."we had liberty in Cairo during the month of Ramadan, the Arab holy days and it was quite hairy. They were finding soldiers stabbed to death in back alleys and we were given very serious warnings about not insulting the Arab religion during those days especially. Each company was ordered to pull MP duty in Cairo for one month and when my turn came I think I had only one day to do. We were walking the streets with a gun - a forty-five, a billy club and a brassard on the arm and our sole purpose was to protect American troops wherever need be. One of the reasons we had to do that was not only to protect ourselves from the Arabs but also from the British soldiers. They weren't too kind to us and the reason we found out later was that when the British were advancing, driving Rommel back, the British troops were told that when they reached the Mareth Line behind which the Germans would be hiding, they were to stop. And the American B-25s in the Ninth Air Force were supposed to bomb the Mareth Line and soften it up. The Germans didn't stop, they kept going and the British rather than stop decided to press their advantage and keep going. However nobody bothered to tell the B-25s about it and they bombed the Mareth Line and the British Eight Army. Although it was a British Army mistake by not announcing the fact that they were there, they took umbrage

146th QM Truck Company

and back in Cairo British soldiers would gang up on an American and beat the daylights out of him and put him in hospital. So there was quite a bit of ill feeling because of that."

After the initial novelty of desert life and Arab culture had been experienced. Of daily seeing the Sphinx and the Pyramids, Garland Coghill remembers…"it got commonplace - just like tall buildings in your own home town."

CHAPTER TWELVE

Benghazi

Benghazi fell on the 19th of November 1942 and the Allied armies found to their surprise that the harbour is almost undamaged and could be used immediately, but the power station has been wrecked by Allied bombing and there is no piped water or working sewerage system, depriving the victors of all basic amenities."

But the Allied armies swept on, westward from Benghazi, increasing the distances and durations for the 146th' convoys which by now had reached the point when it was time to move closer to the action, so with Chris Controwinski..."we moved out of Huckstep. The 3rd Platoon was in Palestine on R&R detail and we based in Benghazi. The 147th was at Huckstep too, we didn't pay too much attention, they went their way and we went ours. By the time they (Eighth Army) got the port in Benghazi open, we were in Tripoli and that port wasn't open so we would go back to Benghazi and pick up bombs and gasoline and haul them to the Tripoli area. I was in the maintenance so didn't go on every convoy. A convoy went out and maybe one or two guys from maintenance went on that particular convoy, they'd come back and it was the next guys turn to go out on the next convoy while we stayed in camp and did any necessary work, cleaned up, wrote letters, read our mail and goofed off in general.

Before Tripoli fell to the Allies the U.S. Ninth Air Force heavy bombers would fly from the Suez Canal zone to refuel and arm at a bleak airstrip just outside Benghazi, called Gambut, before taking off for their targets further west.

On their return to Gambut from those bombing missions, aircrews were

Maintenance crew

fed, de-briefed and then took off for their home bases, leaving Gambut to the swirling desert winds and the neighbouring Senousi Bedouin Arabs.

Now their arrival at Gambut was on a larger, more permanent scale and transformed the one blockhouse, desolate and lonely air strip into a hive of activity as ground crews' service vehicles and ambulances took position and accommodation was prepared for the incoming aircrews.

Casualties were to be received here from squadron aid stations along with Service of Supply patients Gambut airfield by the 1st Platoon of the 4th Field Hospital who operated here from the 29th of January 1943 until they moved forward to Benghazi a month later where they were subsequently relieved by the 15th Field Hospital in mid May.

Once the hospital and Air Force ground support units were ready the 98th and 367th Bomb Groups arrived at El Adem and Gambut, commencing missions against desert targets as well as Sicily, Sardinia and the Italian mainland.

They were joined at the end of June by two 8th Air Force B-24 groups, the 44th and the 98th for the final stages of the pre-invasion bombardment of Sicily.

The 146th were now hauling flat out for the Ninth Air Force whose appetite for bombs, ammunition and fuel seemed to be insatiable as bombing raids, fighter patrols and transport missions were flown almost non-stop.

Fred Cox remembers these..."two airfields we had to service. One of them was the 98th Bomb Group and I can't remember the number of the other one but they had four engine bombers called Liberators, B-24s. They were the planes used on the Ploesti oilfield raid. We hauled those bombs for that. We went down to El Adem, got those bombs off the airfield

Abandoned German dive bomber

and loaded them onto our trucks. We had five one-ton bombs on each truck and we had little two wheeled trailers that we towed behind the trucks and that's where the fins and fuses were. Now the fins were packaged and the fuse was in that fin assembly. First time I put these bombs on I was scared 'bout hitting a bump, but the bomb won't explode without the fuse. But after a mile or two you forget all about what you're hauling and take off and go like hell."

Having arrived on..."the 98th Bomb Group airfield, this one guy, Fred Barker decided he's gonna unload these things in a hurry. So he put it into reverse, backed up pretty fast and jammed the brakes on and one or two of the bombs slid off and banged against each other - Jesus! I thought the whole thing was gonna blow up - it was a big joke to him. He pulled forward and backed up and jammed on the brakes and he unloaded all five of them that quick - I didn't have that kind of nerve myself, I let the crane get them off".

146th in convoy

Hauling bombs continued for some weeks and the 146th drivers would sometimes stop overnight at their airfield destination. Rudy Weber noted ..."the Air Force Bomber Command's Liberators were practising low level flying in preparation for the Ploesti raid. When they flew over our tents they could shake you out of your cots".

This low-level flying training and target practice took place over a full-scale mock-up of the Ploesti oil refineries built out in the desert for aircrews to perfect their low-level, horizontal bombing of a target considered vital to the Axis as it produced thirty five percent of all their petroleum products and was therefore a prime strategic and economic target for the Allies.

The raid, codenamed Operation "Soapsuds" - was to be mounted from the Middle East by the Ninth Air Force reinforced with three additional Heavy Bomber Groups.

This presented servicing and support problems for the additional aircraft so 1,100 personnel were temporarily detached from the "Delta" Base area to reinforce the existing ground crews at Gambut and El Adem.

On Sunday 1st August 1943 at first light one hundred and seventy seven B-24 "Liberators" divided into seven target groups took off from airstrips in the Benghazi area to attack Ploesti - now redesignated Operation "Tidal Wave".

Whilst crews of these aircraft had been practising low level formation flying over the Libyan desert for the past ten days, they and their ground crews were quite unaware that their engines were ingesting desert sand - this factor alone had a catastrophic effect upon the raid when eleven aircraft turned back with mechanical problems almost immediately after take off.

Cold statistics complete the grim story.

Total aircraft to leave bases	177
Total aircraft to turn back	11
Total aircraft over target	164
Losses over target	20
Aircraft crashed on landing after turning back	1
Aircraft lost in sea en route to target	2
Aircraft landed at Malta	3
Aircraft landed at Cyprus	11
Aircraft landed at Sicily	7
Aircraft unaccounted for	32

These figures were revised five days later but still made miserable reading

Aircraft lost or missing in Axis territory due to enemy action	41
Aircraft lost to other causes	5
Aircraft interned in Turkey	7
Personnel killed or missing in action	440
Personnel interned in Turkey	79

Of the surviving aircraft that did limp home, less than forty were still airworthy.

Berger Bankston happened to be at Gambut and..."watched the B-24s come back from Ploesti and some of the planes were badly shot up. There was one plane so badly shot up the pilot was mortally wounded and the co-pilot was dead and the engineer, a Tech Sergeant was flying the plane. He had never taken off or landed a B-24 but he had flown straight and level thanks to the plane commander who let him do that occasionally. He was in contact by radio with the field so they knew he was coming and would make a crash landing. We were all sweating it out watching him come in and when the plane landed it crashed and exploded and everybody on board of course died."

The 146th continued their close association with the Air Force, and Fred Cox whilst serving on temporary attachment at El Adem as an ambulance driver..."had to haul these dead bodies, guys that got killed in a B-25 crash, I had three bodies in mine, there was another ambulance there and they had three bodies in that and I was kinda roped in on the burial detail. The British troops were Indian Sikhs, they wore a turban on their head and seemed like the few I saw was all over six foot, but they dug the beautifullest grave. They'd take the spade and almost looked like the sides of the grave were plastered, so smooth looking. We had the bodies on canvas stretchers and we got 'em out and had them laying beside the graves. The buddies of the plane crews, they were there for the funeral and chaplain said service of course and they left before we actually put the bodies down into the grave. They didn't have any caskets they only had olive green GI blankets pinned around and as we picked 'em up you could hear something rattling, I don't know if it was the identification discs or whether it was bones rattling - it was a kinda eerie feeling for me. We used two ropes and lowered them down into the grave but then I had the unpleasant task of throwing the dirt in on them, and them first few shovelfuls falling on that blanket stretched taut around the body, it made this echoing sound, hollow, almost like you were dropping dirt on a drum."

At the conclusion of his attachment Fred returned to Benghazi and found himself on guard duty..."where the 2nd platoon were camped. I was just strolling around, we didn't walk a post with the rifle on the right shoulder, we used to carry it with a loose sling covering sixteen trucks that were dispersed and several tents - and one man would patrol all of that. Danny Sillers come up and said 'Cahill's corporal of the guard let's shake him up a little bit, shoot your rifle off and holler 'corporal of the guard!' So I did that, I shot up in the air and out come Lieutenant McMaster and he used to carry a snub nosed .38 revolver and had it in his pocket all the time. He'd bin shaving or something, just had his undershirt on and his .38 in his hand wondering what the problem was. I told him I wanted get Cahill's attention, there wasn't nothing wrong - so he went on back to his shaving. Finally Cahill come waddling up there and seemed like he'd been sittin' on a latrine or something I don't know why he took so long to get there. I said 'Daggone! if I'd really needed you I'd a been out of luck wouldn't I!' Sillers had a big laugh about that but Cahill didn't particularly find it funny."

Benghazi was the venue for several unusual experiences for some of the 146th.

Fred Kennel encountered some black South African soldiers in Benghazi and one night..."Sergeant Bello and I visited their camp. We drank with these blacks and got into serious arguments over apartheid and prejudice against blacks in America. I often wonder how we got out alive. One thing that amazed me is that they were better educated than we were, many were college graduates."

Louis Brienza witnessed an unbelievable sight after an ammunition ship blew up in Benghazi harbour..."The British blamed the Arabs for it and rounded up a whole group of them, put them in a field and shot them, as much as to say 'That's what'll happen if you do that again!'."

During the night of 14th/15th June 1943 under the cover of darkness an attempt was made by thirty-nine Italian parachutists to destroy planes of the Ninth Air Force as they sat dispersed on those desert airstrips around Benghazi.

But their hearts weren't in the mission and many started looking for someone to whom they could surrender as soon as they landed.

All soldiers develop their natural humour and a degree of cynicism to fend off the psychological effects of terrifying and horrific incidents of war and there were different ways of releasing those dangerous pressures of the mind. Berger Bankston wrote poetry.

"DEATH OVER BENGHAZI"

On the outskirts of Benghazi I stood that lonely dismal day
Observing the damage that lay before me and the little waifs at play
The thought occurred to me as I stood there looking all around
That but for the grace of the Lord above this might be my home town
Hark the siren is sounding the planes are overhead
These little waifs at play there soon may be lying dead.
The ack-ack starts to chatter as the bombs drop all around
And the shrapnel sounds like raindrops as it patters on the ground.

Company Headquarters eventually moved up to Benghazi bringing Sam McClelland as part of the Headquarters Detachment with it.

Bill Albright well remembers..."Sam McClelland, Regular Army Corporal in Governors Island, New York, before being assigned to the 146th as First Sergeant. Sam was a good friend of mine, we joined the Company about the same time and he was a little confused about the difference between the National Guard organisation and the spit and polish he was accustomed to as part of the Governors Island detachment. I was a little confused because a soldiers life in the Quartermaster Corps Training Regiment was spit and polish but the National Guard soldiers here were a little more informal. Consequently Sam developed a reputation for being good with his fists and was subsequently called 'Slinging Sam' by the way he was able to sling his fists and establish his authority as a First Sergeant."

This was about the same time as his field promotion to become Second Lieutenant. Army protocol required that he be re-assigned to another unit so he was assigned back to Camp Huckstep to join the 404th QM truck Company alongside Bill Albright and Cliff Beasley.

Demands made upon the 146th involved yet further shuffling of personnel as Bill recalls..."They transferred Sandoz to become Commanding Officer of the 146th. In the meantime, moving Sandoz left a vacancy in the 147th and Stan Gertie was promoted from First Lieutenant to Captain and Commanding Officer of 147th. He was a full-blooded American Indian - a very solid officer."

Non-commissioned officers were not exempt from change either - up to this point the 1st Platoon Sergeant was Louis Brienza, the 2nd Platoon Sergeant was Reggie Russell, and John Axselle was the 3rd Platoon Sergeant.

John Axselle had returned from Palestine, rejoined the 146th and..."we hadn't been in Benghazi long, we were going up to Tripoli and I was out lining up the trucks that morning, must have been just light, and Sandoz came walking up to me - 'Sergeant Axselle', I said 'Yessir!' and I thought what the hells he want now - he

Sgts Baker, Russel, Hollet & Rhea

used to drive us crazy, he didn't mean to but he's one of those guys just couldn't stay off your shoulder, and he walked up to me and said 'I want you for First Sergeant.' I said 'Captain, don't you realise that I'm junior?' He said 'Don't make a damn bit of difference. I've watched you the last two weeks, the way you handled the outfit, and as of today you're First Sergeant.' I said 'Yessir' - hell I wasn't going to argue with him."

Rudy Weber's return from Cairo to Benghazi on one occasion was tinged with relief after driving for ..."mile after mile in old worn out trucks and a top speed of 25 miles per hour."

Fred Cox was with him and describes this convoy in more detail..."Italians had been in Eritrea and left a bunch of Fiat ten ton trucks and ten ton, four wheel trailers and they were nearly all wooden. The cab was wood, the body was wood, and they was right hand drive and there was room in the cab for four or five guys to sit on the front seat, that's how wide they was. Somehow they got up from Eritrea to Cairo. This Lieutenant who couldn't make the grade to Captain, well he got the chance to take this bunch of Fiat trucks up to Benghazi, I drove one of them, and we had ten tons on each truck so it made twenty tons per driver. It was 835 miles or something like that from Cairo to Benghazi, he was convoy commander and it took us eight days to get there 'cause we could only average about fifteen, eighteen miles an hour. We hooked a wire to the governor and we could get 22 or 23 miles an hour wide open by pulling the governor wire. We took 'em to be unloaded and that guy's face lit up like lights on a Christmas tree. He had got there successfully with all these trucks, 20 ton to the truck, 835 miles per truck and so you can imagine the ton/miles that he got credit for. That made his day - there wasn't no time he got to be a Captain and it wasn't no time after that he was long gone, I never did know what happened to him. 'Going by the Book' we called him."

Fifty of these captured Fiat trucks and trailers had been re- conditioned by the U.S. Arsenal at Samara in Eritrea and shipped to the Delta area for short haul work between Suez and the Helipolis Quartermaster depot. They were never intended for long distance convoy work at all.

There was another side to the dust and heat of the desert, offering simple pleasures that were appreciated by all and described by Fred Cox..."While At Benghazi we had a chance to swim in the beautiful blue Mediterranean, that water's the prettiest water that I've ever seen, a pale blue and the pure white sand, and the water was so clear that you stand there and looked like you could reach right down and touch your toes it was so clean."

Chris Controwinski also remembers travelling in convoy..."day after day alongside the Mediterranean, there was only one road and the Mediterranean was beautiful. We knew the safe places to spend the night and where to pull off in the sand and go swimming but we were still careful." Which was just as well for the Afrika Korps had laid extensive minefields between the coast road and the beach to prevent any Allied by-pass or enveloping movement.

Sirte road sign

Bathing in the Mediterranean was nearly always safe due to a peculiar, unwritten law, obeyed by Allied and Axis warplanes alike that personnel bathing on the beaches would not be attacked - a mutual appreciation of what was probably the most highly prized form of relaxation.

Convoy work was tedious yet some journeys were livened up by the 146th drivers themselves, who as young men possed that youthful sense of fun and adventure for which the debris of war had a particular attraction - Fred Cox was no exception..."on the way back to Kilo 19 camp we gave a ride to an English soldier just out of hospital and he had a couple of days leave. We stopped alongside the road to eat and gas up the trucks. There were a few shells lying about in the field not too far away, scattered out from each other. Someone gets the idea to shoot at one of them to see if it would detonate. They were probably 77mm and so weren't too big a target but it wasn't very long before someone hit the detonating plug and the brass casing exploded backwards towards the trucks, the poor Tommy was crouched down on the far side of the trucks swearing he would never hitch another ride with Yanks. The next trip we again stopped to eat and gas up. Across the road was a German '88' artillery piece mounted on out-riggers. It was pointed at a hill about a mile away. On the other side of the hill was the Mediterranean Sea, but we couldn't see the water because of the hill. Usually these guns would be spiked and the muzzle blown open so they couldn't be fired. This gun hadn't been spiked so someone suggested firing it. They sighted through the open breech and barrel, turned the wheel cranks and aimed it at the middle of the hill. There were several shells nearby so the gun was loaded and the breech closed and locked. There was some old telephone wire running alongside the road in the ditch that was used for a lanyard cord. The shell took off and hit the hill, throwing up dirt and making a hole where it hit. This was so much fun they decided to do it again. They didn't bother to re-aim the gun, and this time it hit near the top of the hill and ricocheted over the top and on out over the water. Soon British plane came flying over the hill. We didn't know what to expect, but he just turned and went back over the hill. We left there in a hurry needless to say".

German "88"

The 146th had been away from the United States now for over twelve months and Fred Kennel recalls about this time..."Lieutenant McMaster was on a convoy when he and the driver ran off a bridge and the Lieutenant had his back broken, so we thought he'd be going home. Some of the platoon stopped to visit him in hospital a few weeks later on a convoy trip and he said 'You know guys, this is our first anniversary overseas and I was planning a little celebration back at Benghazi I had a couple of bottles of Gin and a couple of bottles of Scotch in my foot locker'. One of the guys said 'Forget it Lieutenant, we broke that open and celebrated last week.' McMaster said 'I knew it you dirty * * *, you couldn't wait for me to die!"

Thoughts of home were always present. Berger Bankston was no exception..."One of the things that happened up in the desert that kinda got our goats a little bit - everybody at home was having gasoline rationed and going through quite a bit of inconvenience because of it - and in order to give us something to do when they thought they we were going to receive a visit from President Roosevelt when he was in that area. They told us to wash our trucks with gasoline, which we did, wasting gasoline while our folks at home were going through all that."

Contact with home for Berger Bankston as well as everyone else was important too, even if the well intentioned efforts of the folks back home were sometimes frustrated..."Whenever we received a package of cookies from home there were no cookies - there were just crumbs. My mother used to send me a packet of "Bull Durham" tobacco which was a loose crumbly type of tobacco which we used in the States to roll your own cigarettes, and I asked her to send the tobacco so I could use it to trade for eggs with the natives, which she did. She would also send me small cans of the same kind of food that I was eating over there! beef stew and that sort of stuff.

Now fully acclimatized to a desert existence, bartering with the Arabs became commonplace, Berger Bankston was among those who..."swopped cigarettes for eggs, we never knew whether they were chicken eggs or buzzard eggs, but they were eggs - they tasted like eggs."

The 146th had been in the desert long enough now to formulate a new existence, and making life as comfortable as possible was at the top of everyone's list including Berger Bankston..."One of the things a soldier learns in wartime is to look after yourself - scrounge - the American soldier was extremely good at that, he could make out. We had these little square petrol cans that we hauled for the British, take about four gallons of petrol. I cut the top off one of these cans, punched some holes in the side put about six inches of sand in it and poured in gasoline and lit it and made a stove. I put my helmet on top of that can and I put some canned evaporated milk in there and shaved a chocolate bar into that milk, and I made hot chocolate. I turned the lid that I had cut off the top of the petrol can over and used the bottom side of it as a grill, and fried the eggs that I had traded for cigarettes with the natives. Had hot chocolate and fried eggs!"

The cooks, including Rudy Weber discovered a few more little tricks to eke out their restricted ingredients..."we had powdered milk for cooking, but powdered milk drink does not whip like whipped cream - but add some lemon crystals and it would whip after a fashion."

Water was the most precious and essential commodity in this cruel environment and the American soldier's ingenuity again ensured a plentiful supply as Rudy Weber remembers..."we were rationed to one quart per man per day, one pint was for personal use and the other pint for the kitchen. Our Maintenance men soon salvaged two wrecked water trailers - one was Free French, the other German. We ran as two separate units and each had their own water trailer so each unit would draw water ration for a full company. There was one water supply where you could take all the water you could carry - this was pure spring water from the mountains between the Egyptian border and Tobruk and we would go many miles out of our way to water up there. There were a few water holes on the desert that had water so salty you couldn't drink it, the salt would close up your throat making it impossible to swallow but we discovered that adding lemon crystals from the lemonade packets of our 'C' ration did make the water drinkable."

The luxury of chilled drinking water is something Rudy Weber also recalls..."one trick to chill water was to wrap a five gallon can of water in burlap or something else that would hold water - soak with water and set it in the sun - the faster the water evaporated the cooler the water became - 'refrigeration by condensation'. The desert gets very cold at night and by burying your canteen in the sand overnight you had cold water come morning - by wrapping it in a blanket, the water stayed cool all day."

It was noticeable that the British went about their war somewhat differently - usually at a more leisurely pace. Fred Cox was..."on the way back from Wheelus airfield there was four trucks of us and a corporal. I was driving the lead truck and here we come to some water, somewhere a dam had broken loose and there was water all across the road, and it was flat so we was goin' to drive on through it - it was only about bumper high. We're meeting a British convoy and the lead thing is like a little pick up truck. We drove on the right side of the road so the driver was against the edge of the road and he had an officer with him - the convoy commander, and he was standing up and had his chest and head through a hole on the roof of the truck and he was waving to me to slow down. British usually went slower than we did in convoy speed and just for a minute I didn't catch that he wanted me to slow down. What's he want me to slow down for? He drives his speed I'll drive mine. My corporal said 'Slow down, slow down' so when he said that I let up off my accelerator and I was doing about fifteen miles an hour in third gear and then I see why this officer was waving at me. I was making a wave of water with my bumper and of course I slowed up the truck, stayed back but the wave kept going. Well that wave went and it hit that pick-up, hit the radiator, went up over the bonnet, hit the windshield, went up over the windshield and hit that officer and water went down that hole and all down the front of him. We're getting up a little bit closer to him now and he's shaking his fist at me and you can imagine what he's calling me!"

Americans were still something of a novelty in the Western Desert, their nationality not always catered for in military establishments as Fred Cox discovered..."Once we stopped by a NAAFI canteen to get some tea and biscuits, also needing to use the toilet facilities. There were two privies. The better looking one had a sign stating 'European Only', the less impressive was labelled 'Non - European'. We chuckled about this as we feigned illiteracy and made use of the "European Only"."

Tea and biscuits were normal fare for British personnel and NAAFI canteens, so the U.S. Quartermaster branch of USAFIME capitalised on the availability of the ingredients by negotiating with the British to obtain flour, sugar and tea from their stores rather than having them shipped from the

Convoy at rest

United States..."thereby releasing valuable shipping space for other items". It made sense to do this, even if the GI's diet was altered, but perhaps they were compensated by those other items that took the form of traditional American foodstuffs.

CHAPTER THIRTEEN

Tripoli

Tripoli fell without a fight. Before dawn on 22nd January 1943 an advance party of the British 11th Hussars had cautiously entered the silent city to find the streets deserted and the port systematically demolished by the retreating Germans.

Tripoli was the chief port of Libya and had witnessed numerous conflicts since its foundation as the city of Oea by the Phoenicians in the 7th century B.C. Perhaps its commercial significance contributing to its sole survival of the three ancient cities that had formed the original African Tripolis - Oea, Leptis Magna and Sabratha. It had survived countless wars but never suffered more than at the hands of the Axis troops when they finally fled the city having wrecked the port, denying its use to the advancing Allied forces.

Bill Albright believes the 146th was..."the first U.S. Army convoy to Tripoli, four days after the British Eighth Army took the city which would put the 2nd Platoon there on 27th January 1943. This convoy originated in Darb el Hagg and I had the job of transporting Major Jacobson in my jeep to Tripoli - he was designated to be the Commanding Officer of SoS activities in Tripoli by USAFIME headquarters in Cairo."

Tripoli road sign

The stride of the 146th remained unchecked as they continued with countless miles of convoy routine, driving back and forth across the desert. One particular journey was brightened for Fred Cox who..."went on this convoy to Tripoli and Bankston got on the same truck and it didn't have any fan belts so we had to use jeep fan belts that would wear down after maybe thirty miles. So the main convoy went on ahead and left him and I to come along. It was a three day trip anyway, and man it was like a vacation - just ourselves - and we'd talk about the old time when we was boys and we I used to play in the woods, playing Robin Hood with home made bows and arrows. Another summer vacation from school we's on the kick about Tarzan, so we'd talk and reminisce about that stuff, about school, some of the girls in school, guys we used to play and have sports with, a couple of 'em we fought with, so we had a leisurely time back to Benghazi."

By way of contrast Berger Bankston experienced the British way of travelling when he was abruptly discharged from a British Field Hospital..."and I said 'Well here I am out in the middle of the Sahara Desert, where do I go and how do I get there?' They said 'Well, that's your problem.' So I had my musette bag with me with my shaving articles and I went out on the only highway across the desert - we called it "U.S. One" - and hitched a ride back to Tripoli. I happened to get a ride on a lorry loaded with some British soldiers. Well we were about a hundred miles from Tripoli I guess and if we had persevered I suppose we could have been there in half a day. It took us five! I have never drunk so much tea in my life. We would not drive over twenty five or thirty miles without stopping to brew tea. In the evening we would stop at a private Italian residence and ask the family to cook us a meal, we would provide the food, they had tins of bully beef and whatever else on the truck they would give it to the woman and ask her to cook 'em a hot meal which they would do gladly because we gave them food for doing it."

As the Eighth Army were approaching the city, Berger Bankston and the rest of the 146th had..."decided not to shave until we got to Tripoli. We finally got there six weeks later after shuttling back and forth over the rear areas and were promptly greeted by air raids which frightened the dickens out of us. They were so regular that you could almost set your watches by them. The Germans were bombing the harbour five times a day beginning at eight o'clock in the morning and ending about five or six o'clock in the evening, seldom at night-except one time."

Returning to Tripoli Fred Cox had been duped into an over-indulgence with Aniset and..."Time it got dark where we were staying I swear I didn't hardly know which end was up! Had to go to the bathroom, went over in the corner there to be out of the way and here goes this air raid, and the British have a most beautiful box barrage of anti-aircraft fire, and the pattern was such that the shells would explode in pinkish red light and almost overlap. But I was under the influence and setting there relieving myself and see that up there and every now and again hear something "thunk" on the ground - a piece of flak from the anti-aircraft shells. I had my helmet on, suppose to protect your head, the alcohol was making me all gung ho brave, and a couple of guys were hiding underneath the trucks. So I finished my business and they were hollering 'Come on get in!' but when you're doing something like that you can't stop. That was my first real experience of being in an air raid and didn't have sense to come in out the rain."

Garland Coghill experienced his first enemy air raid in Tripoli..."Three or four of us were standing outside, talking and this enemy plane came over. Propaganda always called 'em 'Corporal Mueller'. I thought how pretty everything was, just like fireworks. But when the shrapnel started falling - that was another story and we dived for cover in a hurry! Of all the air raids I was in I was always more frightened of the shrapnel than I ever was of the bombs."

This shrapnel from enemy air raids and friendly anti-aircraft fire caused another hazard that Bill Albright discovered..."the streets of Tripoli had a lot of shrapnel on them and in attempting to operate our trucks we found we were picking up that shrapnel causing flat tyres. We had shrapnel falling from the skies that would fall on the trucks while they were parked, penetrating in a couple of cases the hood and smashing into parts of the motor, or the back of the truck might have several pieces of shrapnel in it after a night time raid. Because of this we decided to change our strategy and wait until the streets were cleared of shrapnel to avoid continuing to puncture our tyres. This also involved a change in our bivouac and billeting area. There was an apartment house located fairly close by the port that had been used by military personnel as a billet and this apartment house on the ground floor had corrugated steel sliding doors that permitted parking of the trucks underneath the first living space in the building, so consequently we parked the trucks in this space and pulled the corrugated steel doors down when 'Corporal Mueller' arrived. We thought we were pretty clever to be able to pull the trucks out so they wouldn't be damaged by the shrapnel that accompanied these raids. Unfortunately 'Corporal Mueller' one night made us change our mind in that he dropped three, five hundred pound bombs in the particular area we were billeted. One hit one side of the apartment building, the other hit on the other side of the apartment building and the concussion from the bombs sprang the corrugated steel doors outward so that the doors could not be opened. After detaching the hardware of the doors in order to allow trucks to move out from under the building we vacated that billet as being undesirable and ended up in a billet that had been used by Italian troops, further out from the port area."

Berger Bankston was in Tripoli during..."a heavy rainstorm at night and the Germans decided to come over the Mediterranean at low altitude so that the radar wouldn't pick them up and when they got over Tripoli harbour, went up to bombing altitude and dropped the bombs. The British gunners there on the ack-ack guns to protect the harbour were so sure the Germans would not bomb during a rainstorm that they had all left their guns sites so there was no gunfire during the early part of the raid which caused quite a bit of damage. They sank a British corvette, a Greek tanker loaded with gasoline, an American liberty ship which was loaded with ammunition which burned and exploded for the next three or four days and exploded in such a manner that it looked like a 4th of July firework celebration. The American sailor gun crew on that ship had dinner with us the day before, and those five sailors died during that air raid, burned to death or killed as we stood on the edge of the harbour. The whole harbour was on fire, and we listened to the crew of that ship scream as they died and there was nothing we could do to help them."

Whilst Tripoli remained close to the fighting front line the 146th continued convoying there from the rear areas, each time passing an unusual landmark that was puzzling as to its practical significance in such isolation. Fred Cox describes..."'Marble Arch' straddling the road about 75 or 100 feet up, looks like the Arc de Triomphe in France. The only advantage to it as I could see, it was a little bit wider than the road and if you happen to break down there, there'd be a shady spot."

This imposing landmark, the 'Arco dei Fileni', had been erected on Mussolini's orders in the late 1930's to celebrate the completion of a new highway between Benghazi and Tripoli, near the border between Tripolitania and Cyrenaica and had been dubbed with typical Tommy wit as 'Marble Arch'.

To Berger Bankston..."it was one of our 'goals' when we were up in the desert. 'Goals' like Tobruk, then Benghazi, 'Marble Arch', then Tripoli and so forth, and 'Marble Arch' was quite an experience. It had a huge statue of a man reclining on top of it - it was pretty."

But even this curiosity was marred by war as he discovered..." there were several graves where the German army had buried some of their men. They had the Iron Cross markers on the top of them, and there was one grave that was empty - that had not been used, either didn't have a body to put in it, or had to retreat so rapidly that they didn't have time to bury the man. I remember one time I saw an Italian soldier's feet sticking out an embankment, a sandstorm had uncovered his legs. They had buried him alongside the highway in a shallow grave but it didn't last very long."

Major Jarrett of the U.S. Army Ordnance set out in Mid-November 1942 from Cairo for Mersa Matruh on an intelligence gathering mission concerning enemy munitions, and he also passed numerous groups of isolated graves noting that..."the Germans were quite careful of graves of the fallen - even if he was the enemy. All were neat and tidy and had nicely made crosses."

"Marble Arch" stood astride the 'Via Balbia' which was just about the only route between Cairo's supply depots and the front line. Bill Albright remembers..."this was no Autobahn, the road was pot holed from all the traffic and it would take us driving ten hours a day in order to do 200 miles. The normal time to travel from Cairo to Benghazi was three days, and from Cairo to Tripoli was six days, and these were long days. We drove and we ate and we slept, those were the only activities that filled our days. On return trips to Cairo it became a custom that based upon the assurance of the non-commissioned officers that no-one would get into trouble, we

Marble Arch

always seemed to manage to arrive at the city of Alexandria to spend our last night on the road before returning to Heliopolis. The city was an opportunity to allow a little recreation so to speak to compensate for those mindless days on the road."

In addition to the obvious man made hazards and dangers of the war zone, there was proof that those lectures aboard the 'Aquitania' about Egypt being a dirty place probably had a ring of truth about them as Berger Bankston noticed..."They had a disease in the desert that was carried by rats. We would see signs along the way saying "Diseased area, keep moving, don't stop", and there were large areas of Libya among the olive groves where there seemed to be a lot of this disease."

Louis Brienza & Fred Kennel

Indeed endemic diseases in the population gave most cause for concern to the U.S. Army medical service - malaria, yellow fever, typhus, smallpox, dysentery and all types of venereal disease were rife.

Even the routine of sleeping was hazardous to Berger Bankston..."When we would sleep at night in the desert, we would wake in the morning and have a scorpion in our shoes or while you were sleeping on the ground, you would feel a snake or a lizard crawl across your body, and of course the mosquitoes were pretty bad."

One unpleasant and rare phenomenon of the desert was encountered by Rudy Weber..."in the Benghazi area the locusts were so bad that one swing of a board killed twenty to thirty of them. You couldn't see through your windshield because of them."

This was a harsh land with little to recommend it as a place to eke out an existence and Berger Bankston saw first - hand the poverty and hardship endured by..."The people who lived there in such distress with very little to eat, its a wonder they survived. One night Louis Brienza and I were riding in a truck together and we saw a woman hitch hiking on the side of the road, so we decided to pick her up. She spoke Italian and so did Louis - when we got to her house Brienza asked her how they were making out with food and what have you. She said they had very little, but one of the problems was they had no light, there was no electricity and they had no candles and no lamps. So the next day Louis and I got some corned beef and some other canned food from the mess hall. Sergeant Bello who was our mess Sergeant agreed to give it to us when we explained to him why we wanted it. He also gave us several boxes of candles. So we went to the house that night and she cooked us a meal using the food we had provided and she took every candle in every box, and lit them all over the house. She must have had a hundred candles going at one time. And we were protesting saying 'You're using them all up, save some for later' and she said 'No' they'd been dark for so long, 'this is like Christmas - a holiday'."

On 5th September 1943 the U.S. Ninth Air Force were ordered to England to participate in the campaign of bombing the European continent, and to prepare for their role in the forthcoming invasion of France. Their outstanding combat record in the Middle East was only possible with an adequate supply of fuel, munitions and bombs, a large proportion of which were hauled by the 146th. Their efforts reflect the creditable combat statistics of the Ninth Air Force.

Missions	1060
Sorties	15,184
Bombs dropped	36,629,543 lbs
Enemy aircraft destroyed	666
Ships sunk	109

The 146th continued hauling but for other masters now, often exercising their natural senses of mischief, opportunity and ingenuity - Fred Kennel recounts the story..."of hi-jacking a British convoy while moving along the coast road to a NAAFI. The 146th' trucks infiltrated the NAAFI convoy while on the move. One man got out on the hood of the first truck, climbed in the back of the NAAFI vehicle ahead and passed a crate of beer back to his confederate. This happened all along the line until the English convoy Captain spotted something going on and called the convoy to pull over to the side of the road including us Americans. He complained to our Captain, and threatened him with a military tribunal. Our convoy commander didn't know what was going on, but he was guilty of *passing or infiltrating an Allied convoy*. The British Captain insisted on searching the American trucks for his stolen merchandise but he could find nothing as the rogues had taken the bottles, rolled them up in the tarpaulin behind the cab of each truck, broken up the wooden crates and dropped them off as splinters while moving down the highway. Rudolph Weber provided me with several litres of 'Black Horse' Ale."

Bill Albright benefitted in similar fashion..."when we cleared a shipment of American beer from the railhead at Tobruk and a case of beer somehow found its way to my jeep courtesy of Reggie Russell."

CHAPTER FOURTEEN

Palestine

The U.S. Services of Supply area of operations entitled the "Palestine Area" became USAFIME "Levant" Service Command on 15th August 1943, but was short-lived for once the Axis threat to Palestine diminished, so did activity in this command and it was gradually run down.

During this process "Levant" Service Command headquarters moved from Tel-a-Viv to Camp Tel Litwinsky - an engineering and ordnance repair depot some eight miles away with housing for 4,500 troops under canvas. By October 1943 the 24th Station Hospital was closed, transferring its patients to the 38th General Hospital at Camp Huckstep, the Command thereafter remained in being only until January 1944.

3rd Platoon, 146th QM Truck Company

The 146th first became involved with this Command when Lieutenant Brought - who had been a Platoon Leader and Company Motor Officer - went with the 3rd Platoon to Palestine. He was too remain in the Middle East when the 146th left for Europe.

As the strategic situation changed however the 3rd Platoon's original mission became redundant and they found themselves assigned to general transport duties for the 24th Station Hospital at Camp Tel Litwinsky.

Perched on a small hill overlooking the surrounding countryside it enjoyed the very best of the Mediterranean climate and was an ideal location for convalescing patients who arrived by air and rail from all corners of the theatre of operations.

Rudy Weber went with the 3rd Platoon to Tel-a-Viv where ..."we discovered we had no cooks. Four of us volunteered - we found a tent with British rations and field stoves, no master menu, no Mess Sergeant so we arranged for two men to cook on each twenty four hour shift, changing at noon when we all met and made our menu from the supplies at hand. After two months we were feeding four hundred men in a new mess hall. We received American field stoves just in time to cook our Thanksgiving turkeys flown in from the States and we invited a New Zealand outfit camped across the road from us as a 'thank you' for the hospitality they had shown us on our arrival."

American ingenuity was tested again when Rudy Weber encountered catering problems..."our meat ration from the British was one day mutton and one day beef. Our men hated mutton with a passion so we cooks trimmed all the fat from the mutton, added beef bullion and served it in a tomato sauce - they grumbled but ate it. In a very short time we made a deal with a British unit who took our mutton and gave us their beef".

In fact new friendships were made all the time between the 146th, including Rudy Weber and ..."many British Colonial troops, Australians, New Zealanders, Gurkhas from Nepal, Sikhs, South Africans and Kenyans. It was these Swahili speaking Kenyans that did guard duty at our camp with Italian rifles that couldn't fire but nevertheless the Arabs were afraid of them."

On Rudy's shift..."Abe Yaffe was 1st Cook as a Private First Class, I was a 2nd Cook as a Private and much later we had 3rd and 4th Cooks with two stripes and three stripes but we couldn't get a rating so we asked to be relieved from cooking and returned to driving. We asked for a three day pass for a job well done but were told no three day passes were allowed in the Command so we settled for three one day passes and had a great time in Jerusalem."

So did Fred Cox who drove to Tel-a-Viv to fetch oranges and ..."stayed there four days. During that four days one of the guys, George Cooper - he was in our 3rd Platoon - got a jeep and took us to Jerusalem. At the time I didn't have a religious background and down in the old city of Jerusalem - we went down there with this guide and the four of us walked down these streets but they were more like alleys, so narrow an old donkey come along and you'd have to get up against the wall to keep the donkey from brushing you with the basket each side of the body. So we walked the Stations of the Cross and went to where the cross was supposed to have been standing when Jesus was crucified. There was

Colonial guards in Palestine

some kind of priest had a long black beard and a black headdress who gave me a little speck of like gum 'bout big as your thumb nail with a little speck of something in there and that was supposed to be a piece of the cross. I accepted it and kept it a long time and I felt like I'd made a pilgrimage".

The association of the 146th with Palestine was reinforced upon receipt of orders dated 28th December 1942 calling for the formation of a new Quartermaster Truck Company ..."404th Quartermaster Truck Company is constituted and will be activated at the earliest practicable date at a station within the Middle East, cadre to be furnished by 146th Quartermaster Truck Company".

Bill Albright was recalled from Benghazi to ..."make up a Truck Company from U.S. citizens living in the Middle East. I was sent back to Camp Huckstep and joined Cliff Beasley in the formation and training of that 404th Quartermaster Truck Company, and subsequently led their platoons from Camp Huckstep Quartermaster Depot to resupply the Ninth Air Force in the desert. The majority of the recruits did come from Palestine although we did have some South Africans who happened to be American citizens in the Palestine area, but it was primarily Jewish people who were anxious to get into the war, so it wasn't difficult to recruit the hundred and some men".

He recalls the circumstances at that time ..."the Company Headquarters detachment was still in Cairo with two platoons in the desert and the third in Palestine. The Headquarters Detachment was essentially without a mission apart from the Company Clerk writing "Morning Reports", so Cliff Beasley had nothing to do really and for that reason he was selected to go to Palestine to recruit personnel for the 404th Quartermaster Truck Company and he took John L. Cox with him".

Fred Cox recalls the cadre sent to Palestine comprised of men from..."our company and from the 147th. My first cousin John L. Cox - he was a three stripe section Sergeant in Sergeant Brienza's 1st Platoon - he went 'cause he'd get another stripe. Sergeant Jimmy Campbell was in the 147th and he did the same thing. First Cook Reuben Jenkins, he went up there as Mess Sergeant and a few more guys I knew including Eddy Croce and Abraham Yaffe."

The 404th was officially activated on the 15th of January 1943 at Tel-a-Viv, Palestine and initially assigned to the "Levant" Service Command, Services of Supply, USAFIME, alongside the 3rd Platoon of the 146th.

The British had already drawn upon this eager reserve of manpower in Palestine and formed their "Palestine Regiment" of three battalions - two Jewish and one Arab, but they had missed one individual who became Company Clerk of the 404th. Bill Albright remembers..."his father owned the Mount Carmel winery in Palestine, and we sent him home on a three day pass each month in a 2½ ton GMC 4x4 truck with orders for wine, liqueurs etc., to be purchased at special prices direct from his father's winery."

Palestine was also a popular venue for troops taking leave, Bill Albright and Sam McClelland took a seven day leave there while assigned to the 404th and Bill was surprised to find..."There were a large number of Jewish female refugees in Palestine whose only means of support was by prostitution - Sam McClelland and I were even accosted on the beach one night. There was a concrete boardwalk along Tel-a-Viv beach and the ladies of the night would carry a flashlight and they would hand the flashlight to possible clients and invite them to look them over. This was presumably to comply with blackout conditions."

Sam McClelland and Bill Albright

Ironically, so far from the battlefields, it was here in Palestine that the 146th suffered their one and only overseas casualty through a cruel trick of fate when Theodore Chaney fell asleep in tall grass and an Arab driving a truck ran over his head. Rudy Weber was one of the honour guard at the funeral that accorded Chaney full military honours.

Cheney's funeral

CHAPTER FIFTEEN

Camp Russell B. Huckstep, Egypt

1st November 1943 to 27th February 1944

20th November 1943:

Since the end of September 1943, the British have carried out a hasty, improvised and under-strength campaign to occupy the Greek Dodecanese Islands in the Aegean Sea but have steadily and heavily lost to the Germans. The battered remnants of Allied forces now retreat to the last island in the chain and are evacuated.

28th November 1943:

Roosevelt, Churchill and Stalin meet in Teheran confirming the decision to invade Europe in May 1944 naming General Eisenhower as the Supreme Allied Commander for this operation.

22nd January 1944:

A combined task force of American and British troops land almost unopposed at Anzio but in the following days fail to exploit the weak resistance and push for Rome. This mistake allows the Germans a breathing space to regroup and reinforce their units in the area before delivering massive counter-attacks.

4th February 1944:

The Marshall Islands are finally cleared of all Japanese defenders with relatively few American casualties. This campaign is now typical of the American's Pacific island-hopping tactics which are gathering in pace and success.

When the 146th recalled its platoons from the desert and Palestine to be regrouped for embarkation to England in November 1943, Frank Lechert who had been with the 3rd Platoon in Palestine, filled the official Table of Organisation vacancy of Dispatcher in the 146th, replacing Glenn McIlwee who had left them back in May 1943.

John Axselle had no sooner returned to Camp Huckstep than..."This guy comes around, he came to me, he selected me, and he must have taken ten to fifteen guys out of the outfit - some were maintenance, whatever. And he was putting together a Company from all the outfits in Huckstep and he picked the people he wanted and they were gonna be in this invasion force. I sent all my stuff home, all my personal stuff and I figured I was as good as gone and at the last minute they called it off. They reached a point we were restricted to camp, we couldn't go to Cairo - couldn't do nothing. They didn't tell us where we were going - later found out it was Greece. This must have been three months before we left the Middle East to come to England. It was going to be American and British, Navy and Air Force - a combined force."

Even now the merry-go-round of officers continued. Bill Albright explains..."Captain Beasley came back as the Commanding Officer of the 146th, leaving the 404th. I left the 404th and was promoted to First Lieutenant returning to the 146th. We had a Graves Registration Lieutenant by the name of Meril Kenyon who was assigned to the unit - he was mighty glad to be there having spent his time in the Middle Eastern desert identifying remains of Air Force personnel who were lost on their return flights."

Jim Brown joined the Company too, he'd left the United States with a Replacement Company on 13th October 1943 and befriended a Walt Disney employee called O'Neill who pencil sketched him while they were at sea prior to landing at Oran - a picture he carried throughout the war and still treasures to this day.

Rudy Weber's recall journey was one he never forgot..."when we got word to return to Cairo, we also had to take some Ordnance personnel back. We had no officers, but a Warrant Officer was put in charge who didn't know anything about convoy work. We had a GMC wrecker and two mechanics, a 2½ ton kitchen truck and one cook. A trip like this would normally take about ten days but this road was a two lane macadam road built for civilian traffic - picture it after four years of war with tanks and every other type of equipment using it - it was in real sad shape."

"Now came the nightmare - our drivers were taken to a truck salvage dump where we got 1½ ton British Fords that were fixed up to run. The truck I got had a hood wired on with baling wire, the engine was 50-50, the transmission was shot - you could shift up but not down, all that could be done was to let it stop and start over again. We loaded the trucks with gasoline and hoped it was enough for the whole trip - we estimated about 3 to 3½ tons of gasoline on every truck. the first day I lost a fan belt and was towed until we found a British truck supply center, and in the process of being towed I lost my front bumper. We got a Ford fan belt and had to speed to catch the convoy. I had nine flats that first day by the end of which I developed a radiator leak and was towed the rest of the way. About the same time our cook took sick and was taken to a Field Hospital with suspected food poisoning!"

"He remembered I had cooked in Palestine - so I had another job. The Warrant Officer insisted we make meals like you get at base camp so I talked it over with the cook at the hospital that night and got some tips on cooking. I remember making pancakes and chicken fricassee. I was the only cook and had four Ordnance men for KP. A day ran something like this - up around 3 a.m. make breakfast and ready to serve when the convoy woke up. With breakfast finished the convoy took off. Clean the pots and pans, load the field stoves and supplies on the truck, I was also the driver of the truck! Three men rode in the back and one up front with me. Then tear ass down the road and pass the convoy. Stop and set up the kitchen and start dinner - we made a hot meal. By this time the convoy arrived, ate and left again. Clean up the gear and load the truck and on our way again. Pass the convoy and set up and make supper. Another hot meal with 'soup to nuts'. By this time the convoy arrived which would be about 6.30 p.m. and the meal was ready. We would be done about 11.00 p.m. Next day was the same thing all over again."

"At the end of the trip I asked the Warrant Officer to get my KP men a three day pass for a long and hard trip but he couldn't be bothered so I went to their Company Commander for three day passes for them - and got them! Officers do take recommendations from a Private! I couldn't get a pass because we had no Company officer at Camp Huckstep at this time."

Rudy Weber

Result of strafing

Fred Cox well remembers..."While we were up in the desert, the term *up in the blues* was used by the British to describe the front, which had a blue haze hanging over it from exploding shell fire. You weren't considered to be a true fighting man if you hadn't been *in the blues*'" - the 146th had been there for over fifteen months.

CHAPTER SIXTEEN

At sea s.s.- *Otranto*

27th February to 17th March 1944

8th March 1944:

The expected Japanese offensive in Burma opens around Imphal and Kohima against British and American forces. While the attack is anticipated, the strength and ferocity of it takes the Allies by complete surprise and they are forced to withdraw.

By early 1944 the desert war was all but finished, attention now turning to focus on Europe where it was time to make use of the 146th in the forthcoming campaign about to explode across the map of Europe from the beaches of Normandy.

Fred Cox recalls that..."Right before we left we had to get vaccinated. They gave us a "Good Conduct Medal" and I was so proud of that first medal I ever got. We got issued some rubber bottomed shoes because we were supposed to be going on a British tanker and we had to wear these shoes because

Maintenance prior to embarkation

we weren't to make any sparks. But when we got on the boat it was a passenger liner called the *Otranto* and it had British civilians and British service people from India aboard, it had Italian prisoners under lock up, then they had Americans, the 146th and 147th, and some kind of medical outfit, going with us to England."

Built at Barrow-in-Furness, England in 1925 the *Otranto* was a steam turbine passenger vessel of 20,026 tons that had been owned and operated by the Orient Steam Navigation Company. Named after a small, picturesque Roman port in the south eastern part of Italy, now in time of war she was re-christened simply "Troopship EX-23".

At two-thirty in the morning of February 27th 1944 the 146th departed from Camp Russell B. Huckstep, riding in trucks of the 404th QM Truck Company bound for their port of embarkation at Suez where they climbed the gangways aboard the *Otranto* four hours later.

Albert Shaw joined them shortly afterwards, returning to duty judged as recovered from sickness that had confined him to his quarters. Al Gadow and Willie Wilkinson boarded just after him, so by the time *Otranto* set sail the 146th had aboard one Captain, two First Lieutenants, one Second Lieutenant and one hundred and seven Enlisted Men.

Fred Cox remembers the coast of North Africa receding into the distance as he and the rest of the 146th set sail..."through the Mediterranean. We had a barrage balloon hanging from the ship, and these slow moving two winged planes from a British aircraft carrier - they looked almost like World War One planes - and they would fly round, 'cause they were moving slow they could detect submarines. Then about an hour before dusk they would start burning this darned oil to put up a smoke screen and then the submarine couldn't silhouette us between the sunset. Boy that was nauseous!"

As night fell the 146th had a new skill to master - John Axselle..."laughed like hell at the outfit. They gave 'em hammocks, and had to hang 'em up during the day, and at night in the Mess Hall. Oh I laughed my head off as they would get in - fall out. You know a hammock is a mean damn thing to get into if you don't get it right! But cuss - the first coupla nights trying to get in and stay in, keep from falling out and breaking your neck!"

Fred Cox remembers those hammocks too..."the 146th and the 147th and this medical outfit were all below the decks and there was no place to put a bed, no cots, so they gave us hammocks. We slept up on the deck a lot of us. About five o'clock in the morning, here come this old English sailor, I called him old 'cause if you're twenty years old everybody's old, but he must have been like fifty. He'd say 'Show a leg mates, show a leg!' and at first we didn't know what he's getting at other than he woke us up. Pretty soon here comes a coupla younger sailors with a fire hose washing the deck down and I mean you'd better get your butt up or you gonna get soaking wet!"

John Axselle also befriended that 'old' British sailor during the voyage, and as with most fleeting wartime friendships, exchanged addresses with promises of writing when the war was over.

During their stay in the desert the 146th had acquired a taste for British tea that was continued aboard *Otranto* - Fred Cox remembers at about..."two in the afternoon Dan Sillers got this big pitcher of tea - he called it the 'Otranto Tea Club' - and he'd come back and Johnny Alden, Sillers and some more'd drink this tea."

Fred also came across a young girl passenger called Helen..."who reminded me of my sister when she was about that age. When she was six she used to cut her hair like that, straight across, she had blonde hair and blue eyes like my sister, and I was some kinda homesick."

During their Desert service many changes had taken place within the ranks of the 146th QM Truck Company, best illustrated by the following roster comparison.

NON-COMMISSIONED OFFICERS - SEPTEMBER 30TH 1942 TO MARCH 1ST 1944

		Sep 30th 1942	Platoon/ Section	Promoted/ Transferred	Mar 1st 1944
6889188	MCCLELLAND SAMUEL	1 Sgt		Promoted & Transferred	
33046747	AGNOR MARION D	S Sgt	Supply		S Sgt
20348902	AXELLE JOHN F JR	S Sgt		Promoted	1 Sgt
20348653	BELLO JOHN J	S Sgt	Mess		S Sgt
20348631	BRIENZA LOUIS J	S Sgt	Ptn Sgt		S Sgt
20346632	CRANDALL JOHN M	S Sgt	Promoted		T Sgt
20348647	RUSSELL REGINALD R	S Sgt	Ptn Sgt		S Sgt
20348651	BABBIS NICHOLAS	Sgt	Sec Sgt	Transferred	
33051011	CONWAY LEO F	Sgt	Coy Clerk	Transferred	
20348635	COX JOHN L	Sgt	Sec Sgt		Sgt
20348656	CROFT WILLIAM H	Sgt	Sec Sgt	Transferred	
33009257	JOHNSON GEORGE E	Sgt	Sec Sgt	Promoted	S Sgt
33041920	LAMB RICHARD F	Sgt	Coy Clerk	Transferred	
20348655	CONTROWINSKI CHRIS S	TEC4	Mechanic		TEC4
20348660	JENKINS REUBIN W	TEC4	Cook	Transferred	
20348643	KENNEL FRED E	TEC4	Cook		TEC4
20348662	MATHEWS ROLAND H	TEC4	Mechanic		TEC4
20348668	WARD PAUL P	TEC4		Transferred	
33042087	BAKER LINNIE L	Cpl	Squad Ldr	Promoted	Sgt
20346658	BANKSTON BERGER M	Cpl		Transferred	
33042098	BENNETT ROBERT L	Cpl		Transferred	
33081008	CAHILL THOMAS L	Cpl			Cpl
33041822	COLEMAN JOHN M JR	Cpl		Transferred	
20348658	FORNILL FRICK	Cpl		Promoted	Sgt
33009332	HOLLETT JOHN W	Cpl	Squad Ldr	Promoted	Sgt
20346783	LITTLE FRANCIS E	Cpl	Clerk Typist	Promoted	Sgt
33009294	MCILWEE GLENN M	Cpl	Dispatcher	Transferred	
33009330	PERRY ROBERT D	Cpl	Squad Ldr		Cpl
33041704	RHEA AUBREY A	Cpl		Promoted	Sgt
20348945	SCHERER WALLACE E	Cpl		Promoted	Sgt
33026005	TALIAFERRO HOLLIS V	Cpl			Cpl
33017734	WHITEMAN MARLIN R	Cpl	Squad Ldr		Cpl
20348667	TEAGLE JOHN W	TEC5		Promoted	TEC4
33009301	SIPES MERRILL J	TEC5		Promoted	TEC4
33042106	BEADLES LESLIE C	Pfc		Promoted	Cpl
33050975	BECK EDWARD J	Pfc		Promoted	Cpl
33042234	BERRYMAN LEWIS M	TEC5		Promoted	Cpl
33042023	DENTON BERNARD A	TEC5		Promoted	Cpl
20348911	DUNCAN WALTER R	Pfc		Promoted	Cpl
33009191	KASTINA JOSEPH J	Pfc		Promoted	Cpl
33009144	LANG ALFRED J	Pvt		Promoted	Cpl
33009120	LECHERT FRANK W JR	TEC5		Promoted	Cpl
33048802	MASON TONCHIE Y	TEC5		Promoted	Cpl
34115151	LOUDERMELT SYLVESTER	TEC5		Promoted	Cpl
20348666	SILLERS DANIEL J	TEC5		Promoted	Cpl

As the low, blue North African continent receded over the stern of the *Otranto*, the 146th had time to reflect. Most of them had been away from their homes for more than a year and a half now, they had seen some of their number leave to join other units and they had left others behind. They were in a way sad to leave, but the uncertainty of their future gave rise to an air of excitement and anticipation that temporarily overcame the nostalgia of their desert experience.

CHAPTER SEVENTEEN

Southampton, England

18th March - 16th April 1944

The tide of Axis aggression is on the turn throughout Europe, Russia and in the Pacific as enemy forces suffer successive defeats in all their land campaigns and Allied air superiority gradually takes over the skies in all theatres of operations.

As one consequence of this reversal in the air war, the Allied bomber offensive reaches a new level of intensity as several "thousand bomber" raids are mounted against industrial targets deep inside Germany, and at strategic sites in France in preparation for Operation "Overlord".

The transition from the searing desert heat to the damp English gloom, according to Fred Cox..."took us three weeks to get to Liverpool, and man that old deck got cold but we still slept on the deck the whole time."

John Axselle was delighted to arrive but..."we sat out there in the harbour for a couple of days - it was as foggy as hell - and then we moved in and unloaded, and nothing ever looked so good as those blondes with that real white pale skin! And that green grass!"

The 146th had disembarked from the *Otranto* in Liverpool docks at a quarter past six in the morning of March 18th and with Fred Cox..."rode a train early in the morning and went to London. We had to get off that train and walk to another train that took us to Southampton."

During those train journeys John Axselle was..."mesmerised, I just sat and looked at those green fields - 'cause I'm from a farm and all I seen was desert for eighteen months."

On arrival at Southampton at nine o'clock the same evening, the 146th were met from their train, as Fred Cox recalls, by..."these guys in little 6x6 weapons carriers. They hauled us on out to Mayfield elementary school, Southampton, got there like ten o'clock at night. Always at night when we get to these different places! Finally about one o'clock we got to sleep. About six or six thirty they came waking us up to check if we had any diseases. Before we left Camp Huckstep we had to get vaccinated because we was going to England, and at Liverpool we managed to get vaccinated again - the British did it to make sure it was done properly, they didn't trust American doctors!"

On the 25th March 1944 Special Order Number 62 was issued by the Headquarters 14th Port, Southampton to the 146th authorising travel to London to collect their trucks and the following personnel were selected for the detail.

1st Lt William R Albright	01573003 QMC		
1st Lt William H McMaster	01575461 QMC		
S Sgt Marion D Agnor	33046747	S Sgt Louis J Brienza	20348631
S Sgt George E Johnson	33009257	S Sgt Reginald R Russell	20348647
Sgt Linnie L Baker	33042087	Sgt Frick Fornill	20348658
Sgt John W Hollett	33009332	Sgt Aubrey A Rhea	33041704
Sgt Wallace E Scherer	20348945	Tec 4 Chris Controwinski	20348655
Tec 4 Roland H Mathews	20348662	Tec 4 Merill J Sipes	33009301
Cpl Leslie C Beadles	33042106	Cpl Edward J Beck	33050975
Cpl Lewis H Berryman	33042234	Cpl Thomas L Cahill	33081008
Cpl Bernard A Denton	33042023	Cpl Walter R Duncan	20348911
Cpl Joseph Kastina Jr	33009191	Cpl Sylvester Loudermelt	34115151
Cpl Tonchie Y Mason	33048805	Cpl Robert D Perry	33009330

Cpl Daniel J Sillers	20348666	Cpl Hollis V Taliaferro	35026005
Cpl Marlin R Whiteman	33017734	Tec 5 John J Alden	20348650
Tec 5 Nathan W Angstadt	33077933	Tec 5 Carl J Atkins	33046565
Tec 5 Charles Beadles	20348905	Tec 5 James H Berry	33009370
Tec 5 James W Bryant	20346471	Tec 5 Leon J Budres	32158539
Tec 5 Dennis W Cheeley	33042227	Tec 5 Garland P Coghill	20348957
Tec 5 George M Cooper	33042068	Tec 5 Frederick H Cox	20348671
Tec 5 Jessie W Cox	34142989	Tec 5 William G Disney	20348657
Tec 5 William D Frazer	33009164	Tec 5 Alfred B Gadow	33009327
Tec 5 Wilson W Gee	33042212	Tec 5 Charles R Hamilton	33009362
Tec 5 Clarence S Inman	34143382	Tec 5 Benedict E Jenkins	33009382
Tec 5 Charles M Laker	33009265	Tec 5 William LeStrange	33050995
Tec 5 Stuart E Oliver	20349331	Tec 5 Henry M Parker	34098313
Tec 5 Harry P Stuart	33009141	Tec 5 William E Taylor	33042125
Tec 5 Michael Zemel	33009133	Pfc Fred L Barker	20348904
Pfc Roscoe K Beach	33009156	Pfc William H Chambers	34769332
Pfc Henry R Holt	13014950	Pfc Harry E Longanecker	35384355
Pfc Roscoe J Morasco	32094265	Pfc Solomon Scott	33009109
Pfc Rudolph Weber Jr	33001947	Pfc Frank Zuppardi Jr	32069227
Pvt James L Brown	35753412	Pvt Herman L Burns	35?58?48
Pvt John Commarata	32911090	Pvt Lawrence W Campbell	33635191
Pvt Furey A Campellone	33778482	Pvt Thomas E Carter	34804407
Pvt Henry G Chestnut Jr	34804336	Pvt Spencer H Collins	20348909
Pvt Benjamin F DiSano	31148074	Pvt Paul F Griffin	6929175
Pvt Virgil F Lincks	37106663	Pvt Joseph Savage Jr	32058802
Pvt Kirby J Shutt	19104321	Pvt Elroy W Toppel Jr	20349338
Pvt Jessie A Warvin	20348672		

CHAPTER EIGHTEEN

Dorchester, England

16th April - 2nd June 1944

18th April 1944:

Security measures are further tightened in preparation for Operation "Overlord" as all coded radio and telegraph transmissions from the British Isles are banned. Telephone services and newspaper deliveries to Southern Ireland and Gibraltar have already ceased.

May 1944:

The Allied air offensive switches its main effort from industrial targets in Germany to road and rail communications throughout north western France in preparation for D-Day.

No sooner had they retrieved their trucks from the port of London and returned to Southampton than, as Chris Controwinski succinctly recalls..."We went out in the country and bivouacked alongside the road."

That bivouac site is also remembered by Fred Cox..."Our tents were pitched in a cow pasture about three quarters of a mile from the road leading from Dorchester to Weymouth. There was a rather large oak tree that had blown over and the trunk was lying horizontal and was just high enough off the ground to make a nice stand-up mess table. Some of the roots protruding at the base of the tree were adorned with the after birth of a cow having recently given birth. This did not seem to affect anyones appetite but the first men in the chow line did seem to favour the other end of the tree trunk."

Work soon began, and on one trip Fred Cox and others..."had to go up to these Quonset huts. American Rangers were billeted in them and we loaded these guys up in our trucks and hauled them out. Well we talked - and they told us the reason they was being moved out. There was a black outfit stationed nearby - Negroes. These Negroes beat up a couple of these Rangers and cut 'em. So these Rangers went over to this black outfit and caught about twenty five of 'em in bed and just worked on 'em."

There were always mundane tasks for Fred Cox and his colleagues..."We'd go down to Portland different days and do different little details, or we'd go into Dorchester and pick up the 1st Division at the train station and haul them out to what we called these "D Area" camps nearby around Dorchester, and then we would come on back - each time they left the camps they supposed it was to be the landing in France."

Perhaps the 1st Division troops mistaken belief was based on the timed convoys Rudy Weber remembers when..."we would pick up troops and take them to the docks to load on

Dorchester

ships. We had to be at given check points at precise times to prevent tie-ups, the idea being to keep a continuance of movement to the ships, and away from the docks."

A chance reunion awaited Fred Cox on one detail..."where I was on loan to the American Navy and hauled several Navy personnel to Exeter to pick up some crates of 'what have you'. While there I saw the officer who was my Battalion CO in 1941 when I was in the 29th Division. The trip seemed a leisurely round trip of less than eight hours from Portland where the Navy men were stationed - they were something to do with the Mulberry harbour sections afloat at Portland."

Even at this late stage of the war the Luftwaffe were not a spent force as Fred Kennel recalls, and..."When German planes came over at dark the anti-aircraft opened up - we watched, ready to jump into our slit trenches. Suddenly the gunners scored a direct hit and we all cheered but later found out it was one of our fighters (American) that wasn't supposed to be there."

One enemy night raid did get through, dropping bombs near the bivouac, area throwing Louis Brienza out of bed and peppering tents with shrapnel. In the morning, inspection revealed the railway line from Dorchester to Weymouth had a crater in the middle of it only a couple of hundred yards from their camp. It was supposed the Luftwaffe had got wind of the impending Normandy invasion and were trying to cut lines of communication between the concentration areas and possible ports of embarkation.

During the night of the 27th/28th of April 1944 a blacked out convoy of eight American landing ships crammed with engineer troops of the 1st Engineer Special Brigade heading for a practice landing at Slapton Sands - codenamed "Exercise Tiger" - was steaming at six knots under a dim quarter moon in the calm and windless English Channel to the west of Portland.

Two vessels had been allocated as convoy escort, H.M.S. *Scimitar* and H.M.S. *Azalea* which were the best the Royal Navy would provide so near to D-Day, but *Scimitar* was holed by an LST whilst maneuvering in Plymouth waters and never left port.

Azalea took the convoy out and it wasn't until midnight that the duty ship at Devonport, Plymouth - H.M.S. *Saladin* - was ordered to put to sea to join her as a replacement for *Scimitar*.

At approximately 1.30 am officers on watch aboard the convoy LSTs were alerted by tracer fire to the rear and port side of the convoy, quickly followed by a sighting to starboard of a ship on fire, then two LSTs in the column formation were torpedoed, rolled over and sank within minutes.

H.M.S. *Saladin* had just arrived but was unable to make contact with *Azalea* and did what she could with her single four inch gun, firing inconclusively at what her crew believed to be enemy "S-Boats" darting among the tracer bullets and confusion of a close sea engagement at night.

A group of German fast patrol boats, alerted by an increase in radio traffic in the Channel had indeed set out from Cherbourg on patrol and by chance encountered convoy T4.

They were unable to identify their targets and fearing they were warships, capable of retaliation loosed their torpedoes and roared away into the safety of darkness leaving behind a confused scene of death and destruction the enormity and significance of which would not be discovered until first light.

As dawn broke *Saladin* searched for survivors in the water and picked up as many as she could find, leaving bodies to float at the mercy of the tide, crew members noting that many had life preservers incorrectly positioned around the waist.

Satisfied there were no more survivors, *Saladin* made her way to Portland where her sad load was gently put ashore at about 8.00 a.m.

The first hint of tragedy came to the U.S. Army later the same day. The 605th Graves Registration Company stationed at Banbury and commanded by Captain William C. Bearfield were ordered to send a platoon of men to Portland. They arrived after dark and set about their gruesome task of cataloguing and identifying bodies from "dog-tags" and personal documents in their clothing in field hospital tents under blackout conditions, the only lights available were gas lanterns casting eerie shadows inside the tents, and flashlights on the outside.

The men tasked with processing the bodies were initially told that there had been a bombing raid. About three hundred bodies had been brought in and they had to get their job done before day break. But as they began to process the bodies they were found to be wet, some with life vests on, so they knew the disaster happened on water. As more bodies were brought in - so was the truth.

Bivouacked at Dorchester only a few miles north of Portland, Bill Albright remembers..."being awakened around midnight (28th April) and being introduced to a Quartermaster Corps Major wearing the General Staff metal collar insignia of SHAEF headquarters staff. He enquired about my officer's training and about our units performance in the Middle East Theater. He stated that our unit had been selected to perform a secret 'hush hush' assignment, and that he was selecting me as the Convoy Commander, and he held me accountable for preserving the secrecy of the operation, as far as company officers and men involved in the operation were concerned. We then activated all operational 146th QM Company vehicles, and did a shake down to ensure that all vehicles were equipped with their side stakes, bows, tarpaulin covers and rear tarpaulin curtains. We left our bivouac area about 0200 in the morning, driving with blackout lights and followed the Major to Weymouth. He explained to me that the reason for the secrecy was to ensure good relations between the American and British allies. He stated that the German E boats were able to attack the landing craft exercise, because a British Royal Navy destroyer had abandoned its post and assignment to protect the exercise without being properly relieved by an American destroyer, and as a result the British and American naval staff attached to SHAEF were at each others throats over the incident. The decision to keep the incident secret was to avoid bickering at military staff levels, and also to avoid publicizing the incident for consumption by British and American military and civilians. Certainly the secrecy decision was a correct one, for no amount of finger-pointing could change the disastrous result, and harmony between the Allies was most important in the crucial months which lay ahead."

Louis Brienza remembers the 146th QM Truck Company receiving that..."order to go to an area not far from Weymouth. So did the 147th QM Truck Company and another truck company but I don't recall its name. When we arrived to the area, we were told that we were going to transport dead soldiers to an American cemetery near London. The dead soldiers had been in a training exercise in the English Channel when they were attacked by German E boats. All their craft were destroyed and all the soldiers who were in the water were shot by the Germans. Then the US Army or the US Navy picked them up and took them to a place near Weymouth where they were cleaned up and identified."

Rudy Weber was among those who..."left Dorchester for a beach area. When we arrived it was still dark and there was a strange smell in the air. When we asked about it some soldier told us to look into some very large tents. These tents were very long and when I looked in I saw row on row of dead wrapped in blankets on stretchers. We were told that troops on LSTs were on landing exercises and some German E Boats snuck in and sank some of them then machine-gunned the men in the water. At first light we could make out Navy vessels across the bay - this was the Naval base at Weymouth. We had forty trucks of the 146th, part of the 147th and part of another Trucking Company.

By the chill grey of dawn the 605th Graves Registration platoon had completed their task, finding that although some of the bodies were missing arms and legs, they had seen nothing that resembled bullet wounds.

The trucks were loaded, then according to Bill Albright..."with seven litters placed upon the truckbed floor and six litters resting on the truckbed sides, providing transport for thirteen bodies per truck. There were more bodies to be transported than our company trucks could accommodate so we recommended that the Major call in a platoon from a sister company, the 147th QM Truck Company to accommodate the overflow."

Louis Brienza was..."in charge of forty GMC trucks. I had five hundred and twenty dead soldiers on my trucks. There was a Graves Registration GI on each truck in the back. Everything was covered so no one could know what we were hauling. The 147th QM Truck Company had the same amount of dead soldiers on their trucks."

As the trucks were solemnly loaded Gaylon Priest thought..."I recognised someone I knew from New Jersey who was in the Tank Corps."

Rudy Weber saw the trucks loaded..."two tiers high with a rope down the centre, over the bodies to prevent them from bouncing off the stretchers. A blanket was used as a curtain at the second last bow and a soldier from the Graves Registration in Class 1 uniform with a rifle sat at the back of each truck as Honour Guard.

Once the convoy trucks were loaded, covered and checked, all personnel involved in the operation so far, Graves Registration, Medical, and the drivers were assembled alongside the trucks and given a long talk by a First Lieutenant from General Eisenhower's Office about not letting the enemy know how badly the Allies had suffered as a result of this setback. He then told them the trucks would be travelling as a guarded convoy to Brookwood and that any man would be court martialled if he ever talked about what was on those trucks.

Convoy orders were issued to Bill Albright..."to fully fuel all vehicles, and to be prepared to operate non-stop to our destination, to not communicate with civilians or any military personnel, other than our personnel serving on the assignment. A Military Police motorcycle escort led the convoy from Weymouth over the road route which would take us to Brookwood cemetery in London. As convoy Commander I travelled at the rear of the convoy in my jeep with the kitchen truck and maintenance tow truck just ahead of me. Also in the convoy was an empty truck from the 147th QM Truck Company to be used in the event we had a breakdown and found it necessary to transfer cargo. Fortunately we had no maintenance problems and the convoy arrived at the cemetery about noon."

From a practical point of view Rudy Weber recalls..."This was a large convoy of about seventy trucks and run with tight spacing. It was difficult driving because the speed chosen forced you to shift gears constantly - too slow for one gear and too fast for the next. The MPs patrolled the convoy to keep other traffic out and there was also an MP at each and every intersection on the route to ensure that no truck had to stop. At the end of the trip they told us that ours was the best convoy they ever saw - I remember thinking that these dead deserved it."

Garland Coghill drove on that sad convoy with..."thirteen bodies on my truck, I remember looking at these young boys and it seemed like they were just sleeping with their uniforms and shoes on. Going through towns and villages - seemed very early in the morning - I could see people looking up at the backs of the trucks expecting to see troops or something. All the tarpaulins were closed so they couldn't see anything and we'd see an odd expression on their faces."

After driving through the night Fred Cox recalls..."being at the cemetery after daylight the following morning."

Bill Albright recalls their arrival on..."a nice sunlit day, the litters were unloaded from each truck and placed in rows on the ground to be processed. The bodies were not in any state of decomposition, as they were being processed within twenty four hours of their drowning. The unloading proceeded slowly, truck by truck."

The drivers didn't unload their trucks, but like Rudy Weber..."walked around the cemetery and I was impressed with what I saw. By this time I was alone and came upon a small brick building. Inside was a coffin being made ready for burial and it seemed that this pilot was shot down over the Channel and had been in the water for about a month. No head, just some skin and bones. Sawdust was put in the civilian type coffin and the remains placed on top. On top of this was his uniform. Shirt sleeves in jacket sleeves, shirt tail in trousers, tie tied around shirt collar - just like a man when dressed, with his dog tags pinned to the lapel. This entire experience left me with great respect for the way the Services treated their dead."

Fred Cox walked around the cemetery too, and at..."the morgue of the cemetery we looked in the windows and saw the bodies lying on the tables dressed in green fatigue uniforms. I heard some mention that their hair was still wet from being in the water. I doubt this since the uniforms appeared dry and there was no water on the floor of the morgue. While looking at the bodies that lay on the tables I was impressed by the fact that there were no signs of injuries, but for the pallor of their faces and hands, they could have been asleep. I recall that the bodies that I saw in the morgue were clothed in green fatigue uniforms, on their left shoulders they wore a medium blue rectangular patch embossed with a golden anchor. I had heard this patch signified Combined Operations."

When the trucks had departed, the Graves Registration GIs who had accompanied the convoy stayed at Brookwood for about five days assisting personnel already there to dress all the victims in Class A uniforms and bury them in individual graves. Chaplains of different denominations held services each afternoon for the deceased.

Bill Albright's convoy..."returned to the Dorchester area, arriving back at its bivouac about 2200 hours. It had been a long twenty two hour day without sleep for the 146th QM Truck Company on an assignment that has remained etched in the memories of all personnel who took part in it."

Fred Kennel..."didn't go as I was a cook and had to prepare food for these men when they returned to the bivouac area. They told me of picking up bodies and putting them on stretchers across side rails of each truck. It seemed to me that other Truck Companies were also involved. The 147th Truck Company were called in to assist in transporting the bodies to London, and they carried as many bodies as the 146th. So there had to be well over a thousand dead. There was also another transport unit involved that has never been identified according to the drivers involved who told me that in contradiction to the troops drowning and dying of hypothermia, many of the bodies still had on their life jackets and were perforated with what looked to be .50 calibre shells."

"Passing in Review" - a document briefly commenting on the Graves Registration situation in the United Kingdom, states..."When the Germans sank three troopships off southern England there were some 260 casualties recovered. The total loss was reported at approximately 700."

The more modern Pentagon Public Information sheet on Exercise "Tiger" states..."At least 249 casualties were temporarily interred in the World War I cemetery at Brookwood, England."

Corporal Dan Sillers of the 3rd Platoon, 146th who drove on that convoy and was sworn to secrecy was horrified by what he saw..."I thought the invasion had begun. "

CHAPTER NINETEEN

Bristol, England

2nd June - 13th July 1944

4th June 1944:

In the evening units of the U.S. 88th Division enter Rome which has already been abandoned by the Germans respecting its status as an "open city". The following day an Allied ceremonial parade marking their triumphant entry into the city is but a brief pause in the relentless chase northward of the retreating German army.

6th June 1944:

D-Day! Probably the most momentous day of World War Two when Allied troops mount the greatest amphibious assault in military history, invading Europe over the sands of Normandy to liberate the continent and defeat Hitler's armies in less than twelve months.

Only a few days before D-Day the 146th were unaccountably moved out of their bivouac and sent to Bristol. Rudy Weber believes he knows why..."Our outfit was a unit that no matter what job we were handed, it got done, and well done. We griped a lot about getting tough jobs but when you are dependable you are always the chosen one. Before moving to Bristol we had been assigned to haul an infantry unit into France and we learned later that they had a very high loss of men when they landed on D-Day. One figure was put as high as 70%. Four days before going in on D-Day we were chosen to haul in ADSEC units to hit the beach on July 16th 1944. This time it paid off being the chosen ones."

As their trucks rolled into the city of Bristol, Fred Kennel..."felt sorry for the people when we pulled up and dropped off soldiers to bed in their living rooms."

Particularly when he was treated so well by..."Mrs Williams - she was a queen. She served us tea and biscuits on Sunday morning while we lay on cots in her living room. I'll never forget the Williams family saying 'Fred when the war is over come back, if no-one's home, come in and make yourself at home the door is never locked' - I've never forgotten."

Bill Ibright's recollection of their accommodation was that..."Our billets were in private homes, and in the case of the Company Headquarters was an empty house which was the billet of the First Sergeant and the Headquarters Detachment. When we had been there a short time we received orders to increase our Table of Organisation to 129 Enlisted Men, the idea being that we would be able to operate our trucks for more hours in the day if we had alternate drivers - as it turned out, twenty hours a day. The idea being that the additional men plus our non-commissioned officers would provide sufficient personnel. We received these additional personnel in Bristol. Also I received my

Fred Kennel and friends

invasion assignment. I was called to ADSEC Headquarters and reported to the ADSEC Finance Officer. Here I was told that twenty eight trucks would be needed to transport invasion currency to the Continent and the cargo would be delivered only to the ADSEC officer who I visually met and was introduced to."

As the rest of the Company settled into their billets, Fred Cox felt their enforced presence in British homes was ironic because..."Back in history one of the things that made the colonists want their independence from Britain was the "Quartering Act". In order to keep their budget down the British Redcoats would quarter their troops in private homes. Nearly two hundred years later it's the same thing in reverse! Lend-lease in reverse in a sense 'cause the British government was charging the American government a dollar per day for each soldier and the British civilian was getting twenty cents per day per soldier! We fought against that sort of injustice almost two hundred years ago, now the British are letting us be billeted in their homes!"

The 146th stayed in Bristol for only a few weeks and in May 1944 Fred Cox..."had another birthday. Happened to be my twenty first. I was billeted in 33 Wingfield Road in Lower Knowle with Hermann Burns. They had a spare bedroom and a bed frame in there with springs but no mattress so Burns and I, we rolled our bedrolls out on it, we left them there only when we slept because we had to be ready to go in two hours, so in the morning when we'd get up, roll our bedrolls up and have everything ready to go. Right opposite number 33 was a vacant lot and everybody used to shortcut across that lot and the first house there was the house of Miss Kay Summons and I had to pass by her house every morning and every evening going to and from my billet and she managed to be where she could wave at me or say "Hi", that's how come I got acquainted with her."

Life had not been easy in wartime England with food rationing imposed on the population, their hardship being brought home to Fred Cox when..."John Teagle was the cook and he was staying over to clean up and get some of the stuff ready for breakfast. I was standing talking to him and he said 'Fred, there's a coupla girls out there hollering for you.' So I walked down there and sure enough it was Kay and her girl friend Joan, so Kay had this picture - a portrait. She said 'I thought maybe you'd like to have this.' so I said 'Yea sure.' It was a beautiful picture. John Teagle said 'Bring it here let me see.' So I took it to show him the picture and he said 'Look we got a couple of pork chops left over do you think they would like them?' I said 'Yea I guess so.' 'cause things were kinda rationed there. He got me two thick pieces of bread - wasn't sliced daintily like - and he gave me these two pork chop sandwiches. I thought each one of 'em'd eat them right there maybe, but no, my girlfriend put one in each pocket of her coat and took 'em home to mum and dad."

The trucks were parked some distance from the billets, as Fred Cox recalls..."at a dog race track. From there we did different things. We fixed our trucks, put this waterproofing on 'em so you could drive 'em in water, this took us a couple of days I guess, then we had to drive to this big concrete tank. We drive down in there and test how good our waterproofing job was and drive on out if the thing kept running - which mine did. But we had to just have our underpants on as this water came waist or chest high. Then we drove 'em back to the dog track and parked 'em."

Rudy Weber recalls that waterproofing too..."and training to drive through water about six feet deep. The waterproofing material was putty like, and spark plugs, distributor and all electrical parts were covered. The air cleaner was taken off and a flexible hose about three and a half inches in diameter fastened to the carburettor on one end and tied to the windshield at the other end. Another hose was run from the exhaust pipe to a point well above any water we might have to cross. When driving through water, your left hand was used over the end of the tube to act as a choke - this way you controlled how much air got into the carburettor. The training pits of water forced you to stand while driving. You drove into the pit, stopped at the bottom, then drove out the other side."

Among the newly assigned personnel that were arriving to boost their Table of Organisation Fred Cox..."had this new Lieutenant, his name was Skibaloo or something like that. He was fresh out from the States, he just got out of OCS, a 'ninety day wonder', and he was all gung-ho 'bout this close order drill and physical exercise. So this Lieutenant has his platoon marching up and down the street, roughly thirty two or thirty five men. There's a hill there called "Upper Knowle" by the dog track, it was a steep hill with a pub, but they wouldn't even let us go in there to cool off!"

Fred Cox's new Lieutenant Skobielew..."came up with the idea of this machine gun. We were supposed to learn to strip it down and oil it and deal with it if it jammed, and it was supposed to be for my truck - I never did get a ring mount for it. We finally got the trucks waterproofed and everything so we just sat there and fooled around, put the machine gun back in the crate in the back of the truck. When we was finally going to leave - some of us had been selected from the forty eight trucks - we went down to the Finance, and we were gonna haul these "Invasion Francs", like little coupons in 5 Franc notes and 10 Franc notes, 25's and 50's. A Franc at that time was worth 2 American cents. Those trucks were supposed to have a hundred million dollars worth of these invasion Francs. So each truck had all these incendiary grenades and this machine gun in the box and a coupla boxes of .50 calibre ammunition. Didn't mean a damn thing 'cause I couldn't fire the gun, so it stayed in the crate 'til we got over to France and I don't know what happened to it after that."

CHAPTER TWENTY

Marshalling Area "C", England

13th - 14th July 1944

13th July 1944:

Having fought hard to within two miles of St. Lo, the U.S. First Army is brought to a virtual standstill by hardening German resistance. Heavy fighting for the town continues while plans are drawn up to assault the town and the surrounding area to free the stalled American advance with a massive aerial bombardment- this will be codenamed Operation "Cobra".

When Bill Albright..."left Bristol on the 13th July we travelled to the marshalling area, here I was joined by twenty nine officers from various arms of the service and twenty eight Military Policemen. There being one officer and one MP assigned to each vehicle, and one officer - a Major - assigned to ride in my jeep, making up our convoy of twenty eight trucks."

As of 2.00 p.m. on July 13th those on the ADSEC Finance assignment were detached from the 146th by official orders.

01573003	Albright	1st Lt	33009332	Hollett	Sgt
20348662	Mathews	Tec 4	33050975	Beck	Cpl
33042023	Denton	Cpl	33009164	Frazer	Cpl
35026005	Taliaferro	Cpl	33017734	Whiteman	Cpl
33009370	Berry	Tec 5	20346471	Bryant	Tec 5
32158539	Budres	Tec 5	33042227	Cheeley	Tec 5
20348671	Cox Frederick	Tec 5	34142989	Cox Jessie W	Tec 5
33037021	Dovyak	Tec 5	33009382	Jenkins	Tec 5
37285604	Krivz	Tec 5	32094265	Morasco	Tec 5
20548960	Wilkinson	Tec 5	36557529	Agnew	Pfc
34769332	Chambers	Pfc	13014950	Holt	Pfc
20349338	Toppel	Pfc	34135700	Warren	Pfc
20348904	Barker	Pvt	33635191	Campbell	Pvt
34115151	Loudermelt	Pvt	35592350	Myers	Pvt
32352750	Post	Pvt	19104321	Shutt	Pvt

The remainder of the 146th moved the following day to block "C-18", Marshalling Area "C" outside Southampton and met up with the finance convoy, but Private First Class Zuppardi and Private Paschell had to be left in the U.S. Army's 100th General Hospital as they were sick and unfit for duty.

At the marshalling area outside Southampton John Axselle found..."Those buzz bombs were coming in constantly. First Lieutenant Kenyon and I went out this night to pick up this invasion money and we were sitting in this squad tent waiting for the Finance Officer to come. It was two or three o'clock in the morning and we just settled down. We'd watched 'em all night coming in - that little trail of fire behind 'em. And one of these things came in and we heard it cut off and it went off and man it shook us, and he and I both tried to get under that table at the same time, we hit heads and laughed at each other like two damned fools. Those darned things were coming in there constantly. But that night was a real show, we came out of the nissen huts where we stayed, came out into the cold to stand and watch - just like a firework show - every ten, fifteen minutes."

Fred Cox..."never really got to sleep I don't think 'cause buzz bombs kept coming over. You'd see this red light coming and you'd hear it whoom-whoom-whoom-whoom. It seemed like it was only a hundred feet overhead as it went by and feel the vibration from it. I'd heard the thing was set with a gadget that when the fuel gave out then something would make it circle and come back and land and blow up. So heard this thing coming straight up past Southampton at us, we were watching that thing coming, watching that thing coming, and we were up on a hill. So this thing's coming level! Now whether we high enough up the hill that thing aint going to hit us, whew! You feel like you could reach up and touch it, we all got scared. I lay down beside my truck in a ditch put my hands over my head in case that thing went off, and it did, not long after it went past us."

Fred Kennel..."and two others were given the last liberties before sailing and McMaster asked me to get his girl friend a puppy dog as a memento. I couldn't find a dog for sale anywhere and I wound up at a local pub to make enquiries. I met a chap that owned a hot-house and florist business. He said he couldn't provide a dog but he had plenty of flowers. So after several Guinness stouts we proceeded to his establishment where I said 'What kind of flowers do you have?' He said 'Right at the moment we only have jonquils.' I said 'Well, he gave me three pounds so give me that much in flowers' - I didn't realise that I'd get twelve dozen flowers in a bushel basket. His girlfriend almost died when I delivered them and he almost had a stroke when I told him! She wrote him later and told him it probably cost as much to have them hauled away as he paid for them. Lieutenant McMaster was some character and all the guys thought the world of him and went all out for him."

Loaded with "Invasion Currency", Fred Cox and the trucks..."went on down to Southampton and didn't get on the boat 'til toward afternoon. We backed on the LST, put on the elevator and took us up on the top deck and we anchored down, tied the trucks and trailers down so they couldn't get loose, then they brought on tanks down in the hold, so they closed the doors on the front and raised the ramp and we left the shore and went out in the dark."

CHAPTER TWENTY ONE

At sea - English Channel

15th - 16th July 1944

15th July 1944:

U.S. forces are still engaged in heavy fighting around St. Lo, but take advantage of this period of immobility to regroup their forces. The British are advancing at very heavy cost and it is proving very difficult for any of the Allied armies to break out of the narrow coastal strip behind the invasion beaches.

The 146th were aboard ship for two days, and Fred Cox remembers for both those days..."we were in a fog. Finally got to France at night time again, I swear to God about ten or eleven o'clock at night - everything always happened to me ten or eleven o'clock at night I don't know why. And the first thing as we were pulling up toward the beach there to unload - the first darned thing I see - was a buzz bomb, and of course the anti-aircraft guns on the LSTs plus others on the harbour start shooting at the thing and it seemed none of them hit it. Next thing you know the tanks all had to get out the boat first 'cause we was up on the deck and were the last to get out. We went down in the water but the water wasn't really that deep that it got up in the cab, and we pulled up a little grade getting off the beach between these tapes that marked a safe passage through the mines. I was kinda scared as we come on up there and I remember these tanks being real close to us and we'd almost bump 'em, all you could see was blackout lights."

EUROPE

CHAPTER TWENTY TWO

APO 113, France
16th July 1944

Area T-453, France
17th - 21st July 1944

St Pierre du Mont, France
21st - 29th July 1944

Auville, France
29th July - 21st August 1944

Trevieres, France
21st - 28th August 1944

17th July 1944:

Field Marshal Rommel, German hero of the "Afrika Korps" in the North African desert and mastermind of the Normandy beach defences is seriously wounded in France when his vehicle is strafed by an Allied plane.

20th July 1944:

An assassination attempt on Hitler goes disastrously wrong. The bomb planted in his headquarters at Rastenburg only shakes Hitler, wounding him slightly, and fuelling his mistrust of his own generals, many of whom have plotted against him in this attempted coup.

25th July 1944:

During the opening phase of Operation "Cobra" - a massive aerial bombardment designed to cut a path through the dug in German troops facing the Americans around St. Lo - cloud obscured the target area and some U.S. aircraft bombed short killing 25 and wounding 131 men of the U.S. 30th Division. The following day 350 American fighter bombers began a twenty minute all out attack against the enemy in a narrow path on each side of the Periers - St Lo road to the west of St Lo. Then over 1800 medium and heavy bombers and 500 fighter bombers returned for a second assault. Another short drop occurred when by error of a lead bomber, an entire formation of 35 heavy and 42 medium bombers unleashed their cargo at the wrong place. It was again the 30th Division that received the full force of the short drop. This time 111 men were killed including General Leslie J. McNair, and 490 were wounded.

1st August 1944:

The U.S. Third Army commanded by the flamboyant General Patton becomes operational with the mission of taking Brittany. Striking hard and fast the following day sets the pace of their entire campaign which is conducted in spectacular fashion at breakneck speed.

15th August 1944:

Allied forces invade southern France in Operation "Dragoon" and meeting almost no resistance, rapidly advance northwards.

18th August 1944:

Polish and American units close the "Falaise Gap" at Chambois trapping thousands of German troops who have been compelled to use open roads during daylight in a desperate attempt to escape complete encirclement. But Allied fighter-bombers enjoying complete air superiority have systematically destroyed anything that has dared to move on the roads within the pocket, decimating the retreating German armies.

25th August 1944:

Paris is liberated by the Allies as the German commander surrenders to them, flying in the face of direct orders from Hitler to fight for the city. The French 4th Armoured Division fighting to the south of Paris are brought forward to symbolically enter the city, sharing with other Allied units the glory of a ceremonial parade the following day attended by General Charles de Gaulle.

The 146th Morning report calmly states that on Sunday 16th July 1944..."Unit disembarked on continent and proceeded to Hq., APO 113, US Army." They had now entered their second Theatre of Operations, and original members of the unit who had already been away from their homes and loved ones for twenty one months were now about to plunge into the final campaigns to crush Nazi Germany.

It started quietly enough with Bill Albright's twenty-eight truck convoy of 'Invasion Money' splashing ashore..."and following directions and communications between our military police personnel and the MPs on shore we were directed to Ste. Mere Eglise, to a farmhouse where all the trucks were backed up to a barn and the waterproofed bales of invasion currency were off loaded and stored here at the headquarters of the ADSEC Finance Office."

Fred Cox had conscientiously guarded 'his' invasion money because..."We were ordered to safeguard the money at all costs. To defend or destroy so that it didn't fall into enemy hands because of the effect it would have on the economy."

The only calamity to befall them was at 1500 hours when Private Harry S. Bailim was taken to the 96th Evacuation Hospital.

COMPANY MORNING REPORT   17th July 1944

Station: T-453

RECORD OF EVENTS: Unit proceeded from Hq, APO 113, US Army to T-453 and assigned to 103rd QM Bn Mobile (TC) for duty.

                    1 Captain present
                    1 1st Lt absent
                    1 1st Lt present
                    2 2nd Lts present
                118 EM present for duty
                    31 EM absent

Signed: Clifford M Beasley Captain QMC

Once Bill Albright's 'Finance convoy' had caught up with the rest of the Company at T-453, they operated almost exclusively from dumps immediately behind 'Omaha' beach as Fred Cox recalls..."we usually delivered near the front, many times transferring our load directly to trucks from the armoured and artillery units directly engaged with the enemy. When first we were hauling, the trips were short and at night under blackout conditions hauling mostly ammunition and gasoline."

Gasoline was by far the most important commodity in the early stages of the invasion, and Jim Brown describes how..."A petrol tanker would anchor offshore and the gas would be pumped to a platform and then along a pipe onto the beach itself to smaller lines with water spigots where rows of jerry cans were filled and we picked 'em up from there. One time sea water got in with the gas, so they had to separate it and we had to wait there all day. In the meantime the two lane road both sides was full of GI trucks as far as the eye could see. Nobody moved and here comes a command car - Patton! Had his dog in the car, had his two pearl handled guns on and he got out of the command car and I'm sitting right here, and there he is! He walks up to a Second Lieutenant - he was shaking in his shoes you could see it - and he salutes him and he says 'Who the hell's in charge of this Goddam mess? one Jerry come down here with a plane could wipe out the Goddam army, let's disperse this outfit'. It wasn't over half an hour there wasn't a truck on that highway. That's the closest I got to a General."

Garland Coghill was in the same..."bottleneck, and I don't know how many vehicles was in this thing but everything was stalled and nothing was moving. Then this command car came up the road - it was General Patton."

Hauling ammunition was another major task and one particular variety worried Fred Cox, they..."were shells marked 'CWS' and I was concerned that they contained gas, and if the shells were accidentally ruptured, could I become a victim of my own load? I later learned that smoke, white phosphorous, or star shells could be labelled 'CWS'. This worry, plus watching those two blackout lights on the rear of the truck in front put a strain on you - I smoked cigarettes but you didn't dare light one up."

Only a few days after the landings on "Omaha" beach, St Pierre du Mont had been a rallying point for survivors of the 29th Division to mount an attack along the coast road to relieve the 2nd Ranger Battalion who were fighting for their very lives at Pointe du Hoc.

After the initial bloody success on the beaches, the invading American armies were faced by an increasingly resolute enemy who took every advantage of the Norman countryside - the "Bocage" - slowing the Allied advance to a snail's pace. As a consequence the sights and sounds of war were concentrated into a narrow coastal strip from which the Americans simply could not break free. Trapped alongside the ever swelling ranks of combat units the 146th experienced first hand some of the tragedies that took place.

One evening Bill Albright was..."going to reconnoitre a new bivouac area situated in a large pasture field, and debating as to whether to put Company Headquarters on one corner or another. A difference of opinion arose, Captain Beasley prevailed and the next day when we came back the Company Headquarters tent location that I was advocating had received a direct hit by a bomb."

Louis Brienza recalls that decision to stay put and later that night heard..."somebody hollering 'Gas! Gas!'. Well I had my gas mask, my driver didn't have his and he shouted 'Louis, Louis I haven't got my gas mask!' the Captain said to him 'Don't call him Louis, call him Sergeant'. The next morning we went up to where we were supposed to be and what do you think we found - they dropped a bomb right where my platoon would have been, and the German plane had hit right across the road, exploded up in the trees - they were just kids up in that plane."

In the confusing and uncertain darkness of that same air raid Fred Cox..."and Frank Dovyak crouched in the hole we had dug right beside our pup tent. So after the air raid was over could still hear these small arms and everything seemed to be getting closer. Next thing you know start hearing "Gas attack!" and our sentry he was shooting his three shots, pausing and shooting three hearing "Gas attack!" and our sentry he was shooting his three shots, pausing and shooting three more and ringing that iron triangle thing, so Dovyak and I put our gas masks on. Here comes Virgil Links and he hadn't heard about the gas attack. Next thing you know bullets start zipping through them hedges on top of this earth bank. Later on we found out it was a negro outfit on the next road and they heard all this small arms fire getting closer so they started shooting. When they heard our sentry shooting they thought we was shooting at them and we thought they was shooting at us. Links come over, he's hollering for Frank Dovyak, Dovyak had his gas mask on so he's hollering to Links to put his gas mask on in a muffled voice and Links thought, 'cause I was standing behind Dovyak that I was a German and had taken him prisoner and Links was all set to shoot me. Dovyak had to take his gas mask off and holler "Links don't shoot!" and I'm standing there didn't know what to think, didn't even realise Links was gonna shoot me 'til after Dovyak took his gun away from him."

Frank Dovyak and Fred Cox surveyed the aftermath of that raid the next morning..."there was a German plane that had crashed and blew up. Only thing left of one man was ten or fifteen feet of intestines hanging up in the bushes. We walked down across the field and there was a dead German laying, eyes wide open and staring."

Then Operation "Cobra" broke the stalemate with its massive aerial bombardment. Fred Kennel vividly remembers..."that plane raid around St Lo. The wind was blowing toward the Channel and the anti- aircraft foil was coming down over our camp ten miles behind the front. The first wave of bombers were on target (according to reports). The wind came up stronger and blew smoke and debris back towards the Channel, the second wave dropped their load into smoke which by this time had drifted over our front line troops."

But this ill-fated aerial onslaught did break German resistance at St. Lo, allowing the Americans to break out and make lightning advances, typified in Rudy Weber's recollection..."the tanks and infantry poured through this gap and advanced until they ran out of gas. We would drive right up to the tanks and replenish them from 5 gallon cans of gas and off they went to take more objectives."

On 9th June 1944, Company K of the 29th Division had found the Vire bridge at Auville sur le Vey totally destroyed. After heavy fighting around the broken bridge throughout the night, elements of the 29th Reconnaissance Troop made contact with Company A, 1st Battalion of the 401st Glider Infantry Regiment in the very first tenuous joining of the 'Omaha' and 'Utah' beachheads.

Once the area was relatively secured a Bailey Bridge was erected over the river immediately attracting constant enemy artillery fire as this solitary bridge carried the U.S. 1st Army's Main Supply Route between Carentan and Ste Mere Eglise.

This constant enemy bombardment caused traffic bottlenecks each side of the Bailey bridge until the situation was eased considerably by the U.S. 291st Engineer Combat Battalion constructing a two mile by-pass in only five days. It was alongside this new highway outside Auville that the 146th bivouacked.

From here, Fred Cox remembers..."Some of the guys went down to the Brest peninsula, there was a big change in the tide there so the ships came in and would be left in the mud when the tide went out, so the guys would drive out there and unload off the ships."

It was the 3rd Platoon that went to Plestin les Greves, a small village above a sweeping long curve of sand on the Baie de Lannion, a few miles north east of Morlaix in the Brittany peninsula.

Tom Cahill was on that detail, and after a long search around that area came across his brother in the 2nd Division.

With the breakout at St. Lo, Bill Albright remembers the Company started..."to operate trucks from the beachhead on the 'Red Ball Express' and the trucks were kept moving twenty hours a day utilising the extra drivers that were assigned before the Channel crossing. A portion of the Company under my command instead of following the 'Red Ball' operation were despatched with some supplies to a beachhead near Brest. This beachhead was established to receive supplies and transport them to the troops that were containing the contingent of Germans in Brest. This particular beachhead was operated under the command of a General Hodge who later was the General who captured and secured the Remagen bridge across the Rhine. I assigned George Johnson to be liaison with the General as far as the operation of our trucks was concerned, George functioned as a sort of Beach Master/ Dispatcher to unload the LSTs that were bringing in supplies. I also remember being asked aboard one of the LSTs for a shower and dinner in the mess - very enjoyable! When this beachhead operation was over we returned and resumed the 'Red Ball Express' operation and rejoined the Company on the main highway that the 'Red Ball' operated on, but I continued on the 'Red Ball Express' with the 146th on only one round trip."

Bill Albright was then..."given command of a Truck Company to be formed in Europe, the 4268th QM Truck Company. Lieutenant Ralph Skiebelow, the Coast Artillery officer who had been assigned to the 146th when the increase of Table of Organisation strength took place came with me. We filled the ranks of this new Truck Company from replacement depots where personnel injured in the invasion were assigned ready to come back to active duty. When I formed this Company I took with me to become the Motor Sergeant - Merrill Sipes, I also took with me to become the First Sergeant, Wally Scherer, and another 146er who joined me in this organisation was Hollis Taliafero who became a Platoon Sergeant, previously he had been a Sergeant in the 146th, Danny Sillers became a Corporal in the 4268th. The initial headquarters of the 4268th was in Ramboullet, France close by the Headquarters of the 146th. We later moved to Soissons, France where we transported from the ammunition depot and this concluded my official contacts with the 146th. We would pass one another but that was the last time really that I recall seeing the 146th personnel - on the 'Red Ball Express' route when we'd stop and pass the time of day with whoever might be there. "

The departure of Merril Sipes was a slight shock to Chris Controwinski, for since leaving the United States the Maintenance Section..."didn't have many changes. Jack Crandall was the Motor Sergeant, he was easy going, laid back. Roland Mathews was a heck of a nice guy, pretty good mechanic who would tackle anything. Paul Crabtree, Charles Hamilton. Paul Ward - he was pretty much a loner, Jesse Warvin was short and stout with a nice personality."

A major change for the 146th took place on August 11th 1944, with a slight alteration in its title to the "146th Quartermaster Truck Company (Heavy)" and the issue of new, articulated trucks, but it didn't ruffle Chris Controwinski..."We got tractor/trailers in place of our

Rudy Weber

6x6 GMCs all of a sudden. We had never driven tractor/trailers before but it didn't make much difference."

Those tractor/trailers are remembered by Rudy Weber too..."we had 5 ton tractors with 10 ton trailers which often carried 20 tons!"

Garland Coghill had..."never driven a tractor/trailer before, so we practised around in a field, and the first convoy we went out on it was pitch dark, no moon or anything on a road as wide as the vehicle, and I went off the road and had to have a wrecker pull me off, so we didn't make too much time on that deal!"

Rudy Weber experienced the continuing threat from enemy air raids..."we were hauling artillery ammunition and set up an ammo dump in front of the artillery as the front was advancing so fast. That evening after being unloaded we decided to get a few hours sleep. This location was a series of small fields with high dirt banks around them. Jerry came over that night and blew the dump sky high with us sitting inside! Those high dirt banks saved our hides that night. Next morning the artillery leap-frogged past us. You never drove across the middle of a field, you always stayed on the outside so no tracks could be seen from upstairs."

The 146th moved to yet another temporary bivouac area outside the small village of Trevieres which lies just south of the main coast road linking Bayeux and Carentan immediately behind "Omaha" beach in the shallow Aure valley that the Germans had flooded to deter airborne landings.

It was liberated by American troops on June 10th and was conveniently situated for units arriving off the beaches to temporarily bivouac and await orders to move up to the front lines.

CHAPTER TWENTY THREE

Alencon, France

28th August to 10th September 1944

September 1944:

The Allied need for a Channel port becomes desperate as the German armies collapse, their surviving remnants being pursued eastward at an accelerating pace, requiring more and more supplies to be carried along already stretched lines of supply. This prompts the need for a change in strategy, and all propositions rely upon the availability of supplies, accentuating the need for a port large enough to handle the quantities required. But Boulogne, Calais and Le Havre are still in German hands despite heavy bombing and the most strenuous efforts to dislodge them. General Patton's Army solves their supply needs by simply commandeering supply columns, disregarding their assigned recipient or destination.

The quickening pace of the advance was felt by the 146th who were hardly allowed time to orientate themselves, and Alencon, a country market town famous for its lace and surrounded by oak, beech and fir forests gave only the most fleeting of memories to Chris Controwinski..."I remember we were in a field at Alencon. We wandered around, we were a bunch of damned gipsies, wherever they needed something hauled and they could use a truck company or a few trucks - they sent us there."

A high-level strategic decision had now been taken to pursue the enemy beyond the Seine which meant that 100,000 tons of supplies had to be moved to the Chartres-Dreux area by 1st September. Air and rail transport were only able to haul about 25,000 tons between them which left trucks to move more than 75,000 tons from the St Lo area in seven days.

The "Red Ball" grew from 67 Quartermaster Truck Companies to 132 in five days, operating nearly 6,000 vehicles on the French highways. This included provisional truck companies formed from engineer, heavy artillery, chemical and anti-aircraft troops together with all the vehicles from three infantry divisions which effectively immobilised them, in order to move those supplies forward.

Thus the famous "Red Ball Express" began - round the clock non-stop convoys of trucks of all shapes and sizes thundering along a one-way network of highways across France, giving no respite to overloaded trucks and precious little rest for their drivers.

John Axselle concisely described the "Red Ball", its purpose and weaknesses when he was interviewed by Sergeant Wade Jolly of the U.S. Army Radio Service in France and the transmission was relayed home to Virginia State, U.S.A.

John: "The Red Ball is a trucking system which operates on a two-lane highway. Traffic is permitted in one direction only. It's a streamlined method to push vital supplies from ports and the beaches to the guys in the front lines. There is a continuous stream of loaded trucks headed for the front over one highway, while the empties return to the ports and beaches by another one-way route to again load and head back. The Red Ball carries only priority supplies - gas, oil, food and ammunition."

Jolly: "Do you use a single or double driver plan?"

John: "At the present time we are using single drivers. One group of drivers makes a cycle then we assign another group."

Jolly: "How many miles, on the average is one of the trips?"

John: "Let's see, from here, roughly 410 miles is a round trip. Some of the guys have been on the road around fourteen days because every time they hit our area we have moved and they have to continue on through."

Jolly: "How long a stretch does one of your men drive?"

John: "They usually drive about thirty six hours. When we were operating in the Mediterranean Theater of War it took anywhere from five to fourteen days with a convoy. While in this theater a convoy takes about thirty six hours to make a trip. When we were there we had bed rolls and could sleep right beside our trucks on the roads instead of using a bivouac area as we do here. Incidentally, we did just about all of our own maintenance there. There were no ordnance supply depots along the roads over there as there are here for us to use. The salvaging we got from the wrecks on the road over there."

Jolly: "How about your maintenance now?"

John: "We take care of some of it here."

Jolly: "Have you any trouble getting parts?"

John: "We can't get the parts."

Jolly: "What do you do in that case?"

John: "We turn the trucks over to Ordnance. Ordnance has supply depots along the road in this theater. When the next trip comes for us to go to the beaches we draw parts for replacements then. We would rather have the parts so we could fix the trucks ourselves because we lose time when the trucks have to go to the Ordnance depots to be fixed."

Jolly: "Do you have your own mechanics?"

John: "Yes."

Jolly: "What sort of job do they do?"

John: "They do an exceptionally good job. They rebuild the trucks practically from framework on up you might say."

Jolly: "Were most of these boys mechanics before the Army took them?"

John: "No, at the present time we have two that were mechanics prior to joining Uncle Sam. The rest of them got their training in the States. And one of the guys just has mechanical ability."

Jolly: "How are your living conditions?"

John: "The living conditions here aren't what they might be for the simple reason that we are moving so fast. When the boys go out on a trip they take their equipment with them for when they return the chances are the bivouac area has moved and they have to continue to find where we have moved."

Jolly: "What sort of a job would you say these boys in the Transportation Corps are doing as a whole?"

John: "They are doing a very good job. I guess I'm a little prejudiced."

John believes..."we were in Alencon when the 'Red Ball' started. When we first got to France we couldn't go anywhere. Then when Patton broke out and went to Avranches and Coutances, that's when he needed supplies. That's when the 'Red Ball' started, and every once in a while I'd make a trip around, just to check out and I'm in a truck with a guy named Campbell, red headed boy from south west Virginia, and we were hauling steel mats. You step out of the truck and you were up to your knees in mud, and they had a dozer down there. You'd go in and load up and if you had any trouble the dozer'd start pushing you out."

Jim Brown remembers the mud too..."In a communications warehouse the mud was axle deep, you had a dozer pushing trucks into the warehouse and a crane pulling. The dozer pushed you out when you were loaded - it was a crazy situation until this Colonel ordered a hardtop road to be built. And they used flashlight batteries for hardcore for over half a mile to build this road - I've never seen so many flashlight batteries in my life."

Supplies weren't the only thing the 146th hauled, when Jim Brown..."was on what they called the 'Red Horse'. The 'Red Ball' was for supplies, the 'Red Horse' was for troops. We picked up and went down to Le Havre, pitch dark, you couldn't see nothing - no lights of any kind. Loading troops on the trailers with helmets and packs. You don't drive with lights, there's no-one sitting up front with you, so come daylight they said, well we gotta stop, give the troops a break. So this girl gets out, she's a Colonel! She says 'Alright the girls on this side, the boys on that side. Here was a General Hospital we had picked up, and all those things we were hoisting up in those trucks were women! We didn't know it, the girls didn't say anything, nobody said anything, we just shoved 'em on up and shut the tailgate. I don't know how many nurses we carried but it was a whole damn convoy."

Louis Brienza proudly boasts that..."On the 'Red Ball' we had forty trucks on there all the time, you see the other companies, they didn't have forty trucks on there. We kept ours in good condition and had good mechanics."

John Axselle agrees..."If your truck broke down, call the Ordnance and they'd bring another one and put it in its place and take yours away but that never did work out too well. It started out pretty good but wound up being you got somebody else's garbage in place of your well maintained equipment. So what it boiled down to is our guys had a good tractor and if the brakes were faulty or whatever, they'd live with it until such time as they could get the damned thing fixed. I remember Duncan, one time he made a whole trip without the first brake on his tractor, only thing he had was his trailer brakes."

ADSEC were responsible for keeping the 'Red Ball' rolling and used cub planes to spot vehicle casualties for their Ordnance units to maintain a 24-hour wrecking service.

These Ordnance Automotive Maintenance Companies were given 72 hours to rebuild a complete vehicle from the engine upwards, and could install new engines in four to six hours, a clutch in 45 minutes and a complete transmission in 2 hours.

When Bill Albright was with the 146th, he had always been aware of..."a drivers attitude about 'my truck'."

This personal pride had its practical virtues too as John Axselle points out..."It was our equipment and they were damned proud of it, they maintained it. This was the thing that was gonna get them there and bring 'em back, this is what they had to depend on. This was the heart and soul of the whole organisation in regards to the way they performed."

Fred Cox remembers so much of this period was routine..."just from day to day, follow the leader - 'Let's go'. So the Sergeant gets in the front truck and other trucks follow. After a while you get to know those roads, there was a certain road we'd take if we was going to go up toward the front, and we'd come back on another road, which on the 'Red Ball' was what you supposed to do. The Allies had gotten control of the skies so we ran with headlights and we'd have planes patrolling and also every so often they had a truck in the convoy, they called em "Quad 50s or 30s" and had machine guns in the back like a six wheel weapons carrier to shoot the German planes - but any convoy I was ever in I never saw any German planes. We hauled ammunition, maybe twenty two tons of ammunition, supposed to have been a ten ton trailer and the tractors would have bin a five ton, and brakes were only made for that much extra weight, but going down hills I seen them old brakes smoking, try to gear them down as much as possible but you could actually push the pedal right onto the floorboard and the thing just won't stop when you're loaded like that."

Rudy Weber recalls that routine of the 'Red Ball Express' when..."every day commanders from the 1st, 3rd and 7th Armies would call their needs into headquarters and be evaluated. They in turn called the supply depots at the beach as to who gets what and where to deliver. The "Red Ball" was a system of posted roads with "Red Ball" signs, usually one way if possible and no civilian traffic was allowed on it and M.P.s were posted at cross roads and junctions to wave you in the right direction. A lot of places still had (enemy) stragglers who would shoot at the M.P.s and also us at times. We drove day and night with lights on and went into blackout the last ten miles up to the enemy lines. Our outfit ran as two separate sections each with a wrecker and mechanics and the trucks ran 24 hours a day, 7 days a week. We drove without assistant drivers and were allowed one hour to change drivers, throw off flats etcetera at our Company area situated about halfway on the return leg. We had to make a round trip without sleep, and by the time the front was at the German border the beach was 900 miles behind and then we drove 48 to 54 hours without sleep."

ADSEC - Advance Section, Communications Zone European Theater of Operations - whose responsibility was to supply the advancing armies, took over many of the U.S. First Army installations in mid-June 1944 and then were hardly able to keep up with their progress, moving three times in as many weeks, establishing headquarters and supply installations each time.

The average life of a supply point - more usually termed "railhead" - at this time was between ten and sixteen days, and as a sign of the times the term "railhead" was supplanted by "truckhead", still manned by specialist of Quartermaster Railhead Companies and operating ten miles or so behind the front lines.

The tough routine of the 'Red Ball' was eased somewhat as Chris Controwinski recalls when..."We were based alongside the road at a little town called Ponchartrain which wasn't too far from Versailles which wasn't too far from Paris which didn't mean a damned thing to us because all we did was go around "the loop". We did have good tents, we were supposed to be in pup tents but we stole them and we lived kinda high for the type of outfit we were. And they'd come by and gas up and load up with extra gasoline, and if there was anything good on the trucks like fresh meat or something, we sorta helped ourselves. Wherever we were assigned, we followed the truck in front of us, we didn't know where the hell we were going or what we were doing, we just did what we were told and followed the truck in front and hoped the guy knew where he was going. We went through some rough places at times, and then we'd go back the return route to Rouen, load up again come back the eastern route by our base camp in Ponchartrain and the driver and the assistant driver and the maintenance crew would get off, a fresh driving crew and fresh maintenance crew would take over and they would make a round trip."

It was not uncommon for drivers of other units to report to the MPs that their truck and its load had been "stolen", often under the most mysterious of circumstances, but one curious incident is recalled by Chris Controwinski..."When we were on the "Red Ball" we did have a guy steal a truck out of the convoy, he went to Paris, I think he sold the gasoline by the five gallon can. He had lots of money, he invested in a brothel I don't think he bought it, or get the title to it or get to run it but in a matter of a few days the MPs picked him up."

Fred Cox remembers how all this started..."One of the first loads of gasoline we hauled was up to this field, where we were gonna off load it. We unloaded one trailer or a couple of 6x6s maybe and here come these guys from the artillery or armoured division, but they had short wheelbase trucks and the body wasn't as big so they couldn't haul as much as we could so they started loading off the ground and said "Hell this don't make sense us putting them on the ground then they gotta pick it back up again" so we just backed our trucks up to theirs and slid it off - it was a lot easier. In the meantime we had one truck that they'd unloaded, so three guys went into town with the truck and when they come back we weren't there. What happened, Patton was going so fast that they decided not to even make a dump there, we'd just keep the gas on the trucks and drive closer to the front, and so we did that. These three guys drove around trying to find us, meantime the Company was moving like every week. They couldn't find the Company and I really think they didn't try too hard at first. Toward the last might have been getting scared, but anyhow they was gone more than 21 days so they was considered deserters, and the first two got caught."

When eventually the third man was arrested, Fred Kennel..."and another Sergeant brought him from Paris to his Court Martial."

Fred Cox..."happened to be the guard for him, now I'm supposed to watch this guy not let nothing happen to him 'cause I don't know 'bout the British Army but in the American Army, if you let a prisoner get away you gotta do their time. These other two guys got thirty five years I felt sure he'd get forty or more and there's no way in the world I was gonna do his time. They give him thirty years. The MPs took these other two guys back but I had to take him back for somebody to sign a paper. We delivered him back to the stockade and forgot about him."

On the "Red Ball Express" just about anything was trucked by the 146th, Fred Cox recalls the variety..."I hauled potatoes to a little town called Beauvais, I hauled flour to a bakery some place, I hauled Coca-Cola to Brussells, Belgium when they started up the bottling plant there, I hauled rolls of re-enforcing wire, I hauled metal plates, wood decking, mostly ammo and gasoline, I believe I might have hauled more gasoline than anything."

Among all that day-in, day-out routine odd things happened too, Rudy Weber remembers..."one of our guys captured two Germans near the road entrance to our area. At the time all he had was a flashlight - good thing it was dark!"

Jim Brown came across another personality when he was driving..."up the road to Chartreuse and someone came down the highway with one of those boom trucks - crane trucks. He had been up the road ahead of us and the Germans machine-gunned him, and he turned that thing around and he says 'I don't know how I turned it round but the hell with it. You'd better get those shit wagons out of here, the Germans are coming - and they're shooting!'. We were in Chartreuse in a convoy right after they took it and de Gaulle came walking down the street, he was the tallest son of a gun I ever seen in my life. He was walking down the street to show they had taken over Chartreuse."

Paris was always a favourite with the 146th and Rudy Weber was no exception..."Whenever I had a trip to Paris I never stayed overnight at the Transit Camp on the outskirts of the city, it was an old French cavalry stable and you had to sleep on straw. I always took "Rapid Transit" in the Pigalle section of Paris and found a hotel room. A bed with clean sheets was heaven. Our trip ticket was our pass to be in Paris and the M.P.s were always looking for deserters. They'd seal off a square block and search every room of every house and hotel, I was in a hotel during one of these searches about 2.00 a.m. and they searched my room but I had no problem ."

CHAPTER TWENTY FOUR

Cherisy, France
10th - 11th September 1944

Dreux, France
11th - 19th September 1944

Trappes, France
19th September to 1st November 1944

10th September 1944:

American troops enter Luxembourg and units of the U.S. First Army actually reach German soil. Such is the speed of their advance, the need for a Channel port to maintain their supply needs becomes even more desperate and an almighty onslaught is prepared against Le Havre.

14th September 1944:

The U.S. Seventh Army advancing from the south of France make their first contact with troops fighting in the north of the country and five days later have consolidated their positions sufficiently to come under the command of General Eisenhower.

17th September 1944:

Operation "Market Garden" is begun with three Allied Airborne Divisions parachuting behind the enemy front line to seize and hold five vital river crossings to await the British XXX Corps racing towards them, linking up with each in turn. The U.S. 82nd and 101st Airborne Divisions seize their objectives as planned but the British 1st Airborne Division landing at Arnhem - the furthest objective from the front line - encounter unexpected German forces and their mission is doomed to fail.

18th October 1944:

So heavy are Germany's losses of manpower through successive defeats on all fronts that the nation can no longer sustain a flow of replacements to its still active military formations that are gradually withdrawing to defend their "Fatherland". Consequently a desperate decree is issued that all males between the ages of sixteen and sixty are liable for drafting into the "Volksturm" - the home defence force.

21st October 1944:

At noon the city of Aachen is surrendered to U.S. forces after vicious and costly fighting that has left the city in ruins.

The village of Cherisy sits on the opposite bank of the River Eure to the township of Dreux astride the main road to Paris. About seventy miles south east of Le Havre, the 146th bivouacked here briefly before moving across the river into Dreux.

The town had been taken by the XV Corps of General Patton's Third Army on August 16th in a wide sweep designed to encircle and close the "Falaise Pocket" in the mistaken belief that the inner pincer movement had failed.

Since then the Allied front lines had advanced rapidly beyond the borders of France now, into the Low Countries and even Germany itself following the virtual collapse of the Regular German armies but the 146th were held back to bivouac here and there alongside the "Red Ball" highway to continue their task of convoying supplies to the front line from the Normandy beaches hundreds of miles to the rear.

Gaylon Priest and Jim Brown went together on a detail to La Chapelle driving a truck each, loaded with equipment they were told was for the Belgian resistance movement, and they were routed through Brussels. Arriving in the city at night they were completely undecided as to whether or not the city had been taken by Allied troops. There was no-one on the streets to ask so they drove through the deserted and darkened streets at breakneck speed, knocking the corner off a building at one junction.

At most of their bivouacs so far the 146th had slept in, on, under their trucks or sheltered beneath inadequate pup tents until Gaylon Priest found himself in a position to ease the situation for his buddies. He bartered packs of cigarettes in exchange for enough tents for the whole Company and set off for the Company bivouac area with his booty. But they'd gone - packed up and moved while he was away. He dumped the tents and set off in search of his unit, finally locating them at Rouen.

Their endless hours of driving on the "Red Ball" didn't go unrecognised.

```
              HEADQUARTERS EUROPEAN THEATER
                   UNITED STATES ARMY
            OFFICE OF THE COMMANDING GENERAL


                                          1 October 1944
TO: The Officers and Men of the Red Ball Highway.

     1. In any war, there are two tremendous tasks. That of the combat troops
is to fight the enemy. That of the supply troops is to furnish all the
materiel to insure victory. The faster and farther the combat troops advance
against the foe, the greater becomes the battle of supply.

     2. The menace of the Atlantic has been conquered. Supplies are reaching
the continent in increasing streams. But the battle to get those supplies to
the Front becomes daily of mounting importance.

     3. On the continent, the Red Ball Line is the lifeline between combat
and supply. To it falls the tremendous task of getting vital supplies from
ports and depots to the combat troops, when and where such supplies are
needed, materiel without which the Armies might fail.

     4. To you the drivers and the mechanics and your officers, who keep the
Red Ball vehicles constantly moving, I wish to express my deep appreciation.
You are doing an excellent job.

     5. But the struggle is not yet won, for the enemy still fights. So the
Red Ball must continue the battle it is waging so well, with the knowledge
that each truckload which goes through to the combat forces cannot help but
bring victory closer.

                              /s/ Dwight D. Eisenhower
                              /t/ DWIGHT D. EISENHOWER
                                  General, U.S. Army.
```

1st Ind,

Commanding General, Communications Zone, APO 887, U.S. Army, 10 October 1944

TO: Brigadier General Ewart G. Plank, Commanding, Advance Sector, APO 113, U.S. Army

In forwarding our Theater Commander's commendation to the Officers and men of the Red Ball Highways, I wish to add my personal thanks to each of them for their untiring efforts.

Am mindful of the many hardships encountered in the performance of their duties, which makes me proud of this group who are so successfully maintaining our combat lifelines.

/s/ John C.H. Lee
/t/ JOHN C.H. LEE
Lieutenant General, U.S. Army

2nd Ind.

Commanding General, Adv Sec Com Z, APO 113, US Army, 18 Oct 44
TO: G-4, Trans, PM, Engr, Ord, Signal, this HQ

It is with great pleasure that I transmit General EISENHOWER'S commendation to you for transmittal to your officers and men who, through their combined efforts, initiated the Red Ball project and have been and are devoting long hours toward transportation of vital tonnages forward to our armies. The Advanced Section is extremely proud of the part its men are playing in this tremendous project.

It is requested that you bring to the individual notice of each officer and man participating in this large and successful project the commendation of our Supreme Commander and indorsement of our Commanding General.

/s/Ewart G. Plank
/t/EWART G. PLANK
Brigadier General, USA Commanding

3rd Ind.
Transportation Officer, Adv Sec Com Z, APO 113, US Army, 20 Oct 1944
TO: Commanding Officer,Motor Transport Brigade, TC (Prov), APO 113 US Army

I well realize the excellent job every officer and man engaged in Red Ball Highway activities had been doing. The work put forth has been great, and the success of our mission in supplying combat troops has, in a large part, been due to your efforts.

I send my sincere appreciation for the performance of your personnel.

/s/ R.C. Tripp
/t/ R.C. TRIPP
Colonel, TC
Transportation Officer

4th Ind.

HQ MOTOR TRANSPORT BRIGADE TC (PROV), ADVANCE SECTION COM ZONE, APO 113, U.S. ARMY. 27 October 1944

TO: All officers and Enlisted Men of Organisations Operation Red Ball Highway.

It is indeed a pleasure for me to forward to you the communications from Generals EISENHOWER, LEE, PLANK and Colonel TRIPP. To those of you from the Provisional Truck Regiments who have gone to other duties may this be an acknowledgment of a job well done. To those of you who are continuing on Red Ball or on one of the other express routes may this be a spur to even greater devotion to duty in bringing forward the vital supplies for our combat troops. You are fortunate in being able to participate in the largest truck operation in the history of warfare; an operation which will be recorded as an important element in the success of our armies.

ROSS . WARREN
COLONEL, FA,
Commanding.

DISTRIBUTION; A & D
1ea Prov Trk Regt & Co
1ea O and EM of above orgns

5th Ind.

HEADQUARTERS, 513TH QUARTERMASTER GROUP (TC),APO 350, U.S. ARMY 29 OCTOBER 44

TO: All Officers and EM, All units, this group

You men and officers of the 513th QM Group (TM) Units have delivered more than 25 percent of the Brigade total tonnage on the Red Ball Highway. You deserve all the praise for a job well done. I am proud to have been your leader in this important war effort. Congratulations and thanks to all of you.

HUGH H. TOLMAN
Colonel, QMC
Commanding

CHAPTER TWENTY FIVE

St Etienne du Rouvray, France

1st November 1944 to 27th January 1945

6th November 1944:

Franklin D. Roosevelt is elected for an unprecedented fourth term of office as President of the United States with Harry S. Truman as Vice President.

28th November 1944:

The Belgian port of Antwerp has been repaired and receives the first Allied convoy of ships. The opening of the docks will greatly alleviate the stretched Allied supply position, a fact recognised by the Germans who send waves of buzz bombs into the city but which has little effect upon unloading operations.

16th December 1944:

Hitler mounts a final desperate effort to stem the Allied advance which has virtually ground to a halt due to bad weather and a shortage of vital supplies in the forests of the Ardennes. The enemy's strategic objectives are unclear, although the re-taking of Antwerp is an obvious choice. Such is the ferocity and surprise of their attack through such difficult terrain that they succeed in totally dislocating the western front, panicking complacent army commanders who had erroneously placed "green" troops in an over - extended front line with no substantial reserves in hand.

27th January 1945:

In the Pacific and Far East, Allied forces are now persistently re-taking territory from the Japanese and inflicting heavy losses of men, equipment and shipping on a fanatical opponent who will invariably fight to the very last man.

Rouen has been an inland port since Roman times, the town and docks straddling the steep wooded banks of the meandering Seine valley only a few miles from the Channel port of Le Havre. The ancient town is of particular significance to patriotic Frenchmen for their national heroine Joan of Arc was burned at the stake here by the English on 30th May 1431.

In the southern part of the town, surrounded on three sides by a lazy loop of the river lies the residential suburb of St. Etienne du Rouvray which in 1944 offered an unusual temporary home to the 146th.

After months of their nomadic existence it was a relief to Chris Controwinski when..."we got to Rouen on the Seine river - ocean ships could get up that far and we were billeted in a bombed out building that had been an insane asylum in its day. There were no windows in it, but we set up cots and we put shelter halves - half a pup tent - over the windows to keep the cold and rain out."

Their unusual billet is further described by Rudy Weber..."it was three stories high with a large sun room in the centre and wings on each side with long corridors and small rooms off them. When we arrived our squad had the sun room and the small rooms held two or three men each. "

With hardly time to settle the 146th were hauling from Rouen docks and Fred Cox found that you should never take anything for granted..."Stevedores loaded my truck so I watched them putting these cases on, they're made out of wood and you got so you knew the colour code. Right on the corner they'd have one colour or two colours or a combination, and seemed like green and black was PX supplies - cigarettes. These boxes held fifty cartons of cigarettes and ten packs in a carton. On the black market a case was worth a thousand dollars. We drove on, Sergeant Hollett rode with me and I drove the first truck in the convoy up to Liege, Belgium, pulled into the warehouse and negro troops there unloaded us - a negro Lieutenant in charge of them. They get down to the bottom layer on my truck and the box right in the middle, they picked it up out of there and Lieutenant said to me 'What's the meaning of this soldier?' and the darned box had a hole in it and it was empty, somebody made a small hole big enough to get a carton out. When the guys put 'em on of course that hole was down, I didn't see it. I saw 'em put a box on, I didn't know it was empty. So this negro Lieutenant he's gonna get me for stealing them cigarettes, I didn't know what to think. So Sergeant Hollett came over to the Lieutenant and wanted to know what's the matter, Lieutenant told him about the cigarettes, Sergeant Hollett said to him 'Well Lieutenant that was on the bottom layer, he would have had to unload half the load to get to that one to get cigarettes out of it.' the Lieutenant said 'Yea I guess so' Sergeant said 'Well he was driving the first truck and I bin riding with him, he hasn't had time to unload any to get to that bottom stack, beside that I've known him since 1941 and I happen to know that he's not a thief'."

This was about the time that American cigarettes were in short supply, those available being shipped forward to front-line combat troops leaving rear area Post Exchanges trying to persuade customers to buy captured German cigarettes.

Fred's deficient load was an exception for as Rudy Weber notes..."we became masters at loading trucks. On certain cargoes we were checked three times to make sure the count was right but we still had an 'extra' case."

As the Allied armies pressed forward, demoralised German soldiers surrendered themselves in large dejected groups and the sight of enemy prisoners of war moving freely about the rear areas had become commonplace, a few even working - officially and unofficially - for their captors as a means of ensuring personal survival in a war ravaged country that had no means of sustaining them as John Axselle remembers..."we had twelve or fifteen of 'em and there was this little biddy guy we called 'Pop' and he helped Fred Kennel round the kitchen, and there was also this other guy - he was a German Youth, 'SS', the perfect Aryan - and they had a sergeant from the Wehrmacht. He was afraid of him! It was political you see, he was a Nazi and he'd tell 'em not to do this and not to do that. We'd let 'em write home once in a while on a 'V' letter, and this guy had torn up this little guy's letter because it was something he didn't approve of, well - Kennel came to me about it and I carried the Nazi out in front of his group and I told 'em not to pay any attention to anything he said, and if he did say anything, let me know. And from then on they didn't want to leave us, they called me 'Spitzer' or whatever they called a First Sergeant and one of them wanted to be my chauffeur after the war! They were good people although the next move we made we had to give 'em up."

Not only did the 146th make practical use of these men but they were also often tasked with hauling German PoWs. Rudy Weber and Jim Brown recall being on a convoy with seventy to eighty prisoners in each trailer. Travelling from Reims to Dusseldorf, as they drove through the deserted towns and villages, prisoners would bang on the side of the truck for the driver to slow down and they would then jump off the still moving truck in their home towns.

On another PoW haul, while negotiating a sharp corner the stake side of a forty foot trailer collapsed under the weight of the standing men and many fell out. On another such trip a PoW who climbed up the side of the trailer was decapitated by a low slung cable straddling the street.

Roughly a week before Christmas Fred Cox recalls..."some of our fellas went on a convoy up to a big French base outside of Metz, and the 26th "Yankee" Division was back for R & R in this camp and our fellas hauled Christmas mail up to them. They had taken all of our carbines away from us and locked 'em in the supply room, 'cause we were just doing these local details and the Germans were so far away that we wouldn't need to carry our carbines unless we were going to go up close to the front. So these guys who hauled the Christmas mail didn't even take their carbines with 'em. They got up there and the Battle of the Bulge broke out and they were trapped. Next day we came back because we were no longer needed, meanwhile the guys who were up there before we come up to relieve em, they'd hauled the 26th Division back up toward the front to help out and try to relieve Bastogne."

But in the whole of this sector of the battle front there were no reserve units at all to respond to pleas for assistance from the American front line units confused by the complete surprise of the German offensive. Such was the speed of the enemy's westward advance that whole groups of American soldiers were cut off and captured or killed before they could even inform higher headquarters of their predicament, giving rise to a dangerously false and incomplete picture of the German's positions or intentions for those sent to reinforce the 'Bulge'.

Confusion and mistrust was heightened by half true rumours that reached Fred Cox's ears..."well the Germans had put on American uniforms and supposedly parachuted behind the lines and they would take over MP posts and try to direct you into a trap or something so you could be captured or the vehicles destroyed. So the real American MPs set up check points every so often and they would ask you a password or identification or ask you questions that a German wouldn't know. They'd ask some oddball question like who won the World Series, well the Germans wouldn't know which teams were even playing."

Reinforcements had to be found to stem the threatening tide of German success and it fell to the 82nd and 101st U.S. Airborne Divisions who were still licking their wounds after combat in support of the beleaguered British and Polish paratroops at Arnhem, when Rudy Weber remembers the..."call to pick up Airborne troops commanded by General McAuliffe and take them to Bastogne."

Chris Controwinski was on one of the..."ten trucks, Louis Brienza was the Platoon Sergeant on the front and someone was leading him because there were other vehicles, lots of vehicles in this. I was on the maintenance in the last truck as a standby driver, I'd taken a box of tools and a couple of fan belts and some spark plugs - and a wrecker wasn't allowed on this. We drove all night, I don't know where we picked up these troops, I know we went through Sedan and we were going up towards Bastogne.

Louis Brienza..."went up to Sedan to pick up the 82nd and it was snowing, and we covered 'em up with the tarp. We started driving and they had a telephone booth alongside the road, so when I see the guard up there we said 'Chesterfield cigarettes' - 'Go right ahead' So we did, up to Bastogne. Just as we got there they start shooting at us and the guys in the back of my truck start shooting back right through the tarp. So we went back to the guard and he said 'I don't remember sending you up there'. We went down another road and six o'clock in the morning all hell broke loose. They were shooting at each other right over our heads."

Rudy Weber dropped off his 82nd paratroopers..."and right away they start digging foxholes right alongside the road. The guys I had on my truck, I dropped 'em off in the country and you could hear small arms fire. They said the Germans are just over this little hill here."

John Axselle knew the urgency of this haul because..."On this convoy just about everything available went out, it was one of those Go-Go-Go situations. After the deal was over I remember the guys picking up grenades from the back of the trucks, they'd come unhooked from a guys web belt on that haul - they were packed in like cattle, standing all the way, and the tractors and trailers were pitching on them icy roads."

Bill Albright, now with the 4268th QM Truck Company..."brought up the 101st from Soissons. Bastogne was already encircled when we made the trip. I don't think those Airborne boys really enjoyed their trip because they were standing up."

Once the 146th had delivered their troops John Axselle remembers..."the MPs had to wake the drivers up, they were dead beat from hauling these guys in and they'd pull up on the side of the road to get a little sleep and an MP come along and butted a carbine on the cab door 'You'd better get that shit wagon outa here the Germans are coming' and they would hear the tanks, so they left!"

After daybreak Rudy Weber was told..."that Bastogne and the troops we hauled in were completely surrounded. "

In January 1945 Rudy Weber..."hauled in another Airborne unit. These men had spent Christmas in the States and were green troops."

This journey was no better. Chris Controwinski estimates..."we got within ten miles of Bastogne, and we hauled these troops on the back of these trucks. It was below freezing and of course us guys were pretty well dressed and they were in there like cattle. I talked to these people and they said they were the 17th Airborne Division, never been in combat and this was their baptism of fire when they got where they were going. We drove all night 'til just around daylight and they said "Alright this is it!" they told the troops to get out, "unload, get over there, disperse in this area, start to dig yourselves foxholes" And we're there with our trucks I don't know where the rest of 'em went to different places. We lined up there like a bunch of damned fools along the road, ten trucks in the road, some Colonel comes along and he says "Get the hell outa here!". Louis says "We're looking for something to eat for my men, some breakfast" He says "You damned fool get the hell outa here, they got enough targets to shoot at, you just gonna draw fire on us, forget breakfast!". So we forgot breakfast got in the trucks and went down the road as far as we could as fast as we could."

Fred Cox also heard men ..."of the 17th Airborne complaining that their first time in battle and they weren't jumping out of a plane, but riding in a manure wagon!"

For a few anxious weeks the 'Battle of the Bulge' raged through the Ardennes forests but the German's were unable to sustain their aggressive efforts against heroic pockets of American resistance and the line was gradually re-established, forever dashing Hitler's hopes of winning the war.

The appalling weather continued into 1945 and Fred Cox set out from Rouen for..."Antwerp, Belgium and hauled some Americans just got off a ship up there. It had snowed and got on the road from Rouen, had our chains on and got towards Antwerp we took the chains off 'cause the road was clear. We got up to Antwerp that night and we was gettin' these guys loaded on and it was dark and started snowing, we started out and had to stop and put the chains back on again, and these guys fresh from the States was afraid of lights and smoking cigarettes and everything - they were afraid the Germans going to see us - these guys were scared to death! We drove all that night after we got the chains on and it was daylight when we got to this camp called "Camp Lucky Strike". We ate here then we drove on back to Rouen."

Although the 146th had been on the European continent for over six months now, contact with the people of France was quite rare, yet Fred Cox had a charming encounter..."Living in this insane asylum there was an old Frenchman, his wife and little daughter, she was about eight or nine years old. He was the caretaker and he was trying to straighten the place up, there was damage outside, rubble and he separated the bricks from the mortar and stacked the bricks. His wife used to wash clothes for us, she'd iron those old dungaree fatigue clothes. One day not too long before we left the little girl gave me a little card with a picture of the Virgin Mary with a bit of a verse on it she had written in pencil. "Souvenir pour vous, Francine" I still have that card to this day. This was one of the bright spots - one of the memories you cherish."

Destinations grew further and further away from Rouen and John Axselle..."one time went up to Liege - I took a convoy up there, we had gas masks and chemical warfare stuff and this was winter time and the snow was deep and these damned V2 rockets were coming in there - we stopped in Liege, went to the MP Hq there to find out where this outfit was. Out of town they had an old abandoned mine shaft - that's where they were storing the stuff. Got in a jeep, told the guys not to screw off, be right back and we'd move out. Guy named Vanover from West Virginia, he said 'By God Sarge I can't go much further, that truck of mine is missing.' I said 'Well we haven't got much further to go.' He said 'Well I ain't gonna be able to make it.' We went down the street about two blocks, past a theater, made a right, about two more blocks - over there's the MP Hq. Went in, talked with 'em - they told us exactly how to get there. Well, while we were there, one of those damned things came in and knocked us right on our butts. It hit real close. We turned around and came back and the cinema was no longer there, that's where it hit. And when I get back to that convoy they told me they all crowded in a cafe to get a shot of cognac when this thing hit and jammed the door! This guy Vanover - we nicknamed him 'Hangover' - I said to him 'Well Hangover I guess we'll have to leave you'. 'No by God Sarge if it won't run I'll push the S-o-B, I'm not gonna stay in this town!'"

The time came to move on, but one more task awaited Fred Cox..."When we got to leave Rouen we hauled these little things I believe they called 'em "Weasels" for the Canadian Army. They was a little metal box had a caterpillar tread on 'em 'bout the size of an American jeep. We put two of these things on each trailer and we hauled 'em for the Canadian Army at Maastricht, Holland and they was gonna jump off from there I think toward the Rhine. Snow was on the roads when we left Rouen and one truck wrecked and for some reason I wound up taking these few guys to Antwerp, Belgium to pick up a new tractor and trailer and came back to Brussells and spent the night in a transit billet. During the night we kept hearing this thunder and it was them daggone V2's. When I found out what was causing it I was damned glad to get out of there, we come on out of there to the safety of the front. We didn't go into Maastricht, we went straight on into Germany. "

Rudy Weber also remembers those 'Weasels'..."The run to Belgium was marked with yellow diamonds and the roads were mountainous like a steep roller coaster. One icy night we were hauling two 'Weasels' on each trailer, and the road being icy, one truck didn't make a turn and wound up in a deep ditch with a stream. The trailer was still on top but the tractor was at right angles, nose down in the ditch. We left the driver with the truck and took off. That night a lady nearby took him in and although she had four small children shared what little she had. Next day on our return, my truck, Lieutenant McMaster and the wrecker with the maintenance men stayed with the damaged truck and we stayed the night with this same lady. She made a hot meal from our 'Ten-in-One' rations and when we left we gave her all the food we had. The next morning I backed my trailer up and we put the 'Weasels' on my trailer. There were tall trees on the edge of the bank and with block and tackle from the trees to the front bumper the tractor was raised to a horizontal position with the trailer. With block and tackle between my truck and the other trailer I would back my tractor up, slowly pulling the damaged truck back onto the road. I don't remember how many times we had to re-position the block and tackle but for every ten feet I moved, the other truck moved one foot. Once we had the damaged tractor on the road it was towed back and I started back to Belgium with the two 'Weasels'."

The European winter of 1944/45 was bitter and road conditions were worse than treacherous as Rudy Weber sums up..."It was icy to the point that when you stopped, the tractor and trailer slid sideways just from the pitch of the road - you couldn't walk on it, you crawled. "

CHAPTER TWENTY SIX

Ghent, Belgium

27th January - 3rd March 1945

Mons, Belgium

3rd March - 1st April 1945

27th January 1945:

Nearly all gains made by the German's Ardennes offensive have been eliminated and the Allied advance into Germany takes off on a broad front towards the River Rhine.

4th February 1945:

At the Yalta Conference with the war not yet won, Roosevelt, Stalin and Churchill agree upon the division of Germany into occupied zones for each of the four major powers.

7th March 1945:

Tanks of the U.S. Ninth Armoured Division reach the Ludendorff bridge spanning the Rhine at Remagen. Damaged but still standing it is captured intact allowing tanks, troops and equipment to pour across until March 17th when it finally collapses. An alternative crossing has already been built and proudly displays a sign at the western bank declaring :-

THE LONGEST TACTICAL BRIDGE BUILT
FIRST ACROSS THE RHINE
CONSTRUCTED BY 291ST ENGR C BN, 988 TDWY CO, 998 TDWY CO.

24th March 1945:

The Rhine is crossed by American, British and Canadian units on a broad front who are easily able to establish a five mile deep bridgehead on the far side. From now on they will encounter the results of Hitler's scorched earth policy as his bedraggled armies withdraw deeper and deeper into Germany.

1st April 1945:

The largest naval operation in the Pacific, Operation "Iceberg", the invasion of Okinawa begins and meets almost no resistance. The Japanese defending force of an estimated 130,000 troops are believed to be in concealed positions to the south of the American's landing areas.

Garland Coghill..."went to Antwerp, and the city was devastated. Didn't have one window left in any of the buildings, it had been destroyed by the 'buzz bombs' and it was always a relief to see them go ahead of you knowing they wouldn't land where you were."

Garland was an accomplished bass player of some renown, and when Special Services put on a show in Antwerp, among the ruins and devastation they somehow managed to find him one so he could play for them.

While Fred Cox was there..."we unloaded some ships pulled up against the dock and drove up to the edge and then with these electric cranes that travelled on rails they would straddle the truck and pick up these assault boats that were in two parts. They were like two metal boxes with open tops, and the shorter rear half had the engine and it bolted to the longer front half and it was slanted so it could run up on the beach. These metal boxes had little protrusions that aligned and put a bolt through it and made one complete thing. We drove these prime movers and Lowboy trailers and we spent a couple of days or so unloading these ships, there were six or eight of us I guess driving these prime movers towing these Lowboys around. We'd get loaded then drive on round to an open field where they had a crawler crane that would unload 'em. And we thought maybe we'd get the nice job of driving them things up to the front, they was gonna use these to go cross the Rhine. Sometimes when you're on a detached detail like that you kinda get the best of things, and sometimes you get the worst too! We did that for a while when we was in Ghent, and Ghent has these canals in it and the bridges, as the canal boats come down seemed like they had priority and you had to stop and let the bridge swing around or open up to let these canal boats through."

Gaylon Priest and Jim Brown drove to Brussels on one detail, and to justify an overnight stay were provided with a letter of authority:-

---

```
          SUPREME HEADQUARTERS
       ALLIED EXPEDITIONARY FORCE
            MISSION (BELGIUM)

To:   The Town Mayor (U.S.)
      Brussels

      This is to certify that U.S. Trucks No. 556398 & 556189
      (Drivers BROWN & PRIEST) are unable to unload tonight.

You are requested to provide accommodation for the crews, and
garage facilities for the vehicles.

              F S Portal Capt.

29 Jan 45.        SHAEF Mission (Belgium)
```

Fred Cox went for a drink with..."Corporal Mason, my Corporal in charge of third squad, second platoon. He and I was quite good buddies I'd bin with him from the desert in his squad in January '43. He and I was in Ghent in a nice restaurant and night club. They had an orchestra there, and he and I were drinking with another guy - Thompson. Sergeant Axselle for some reason we thought was mad at us and we thought we was gonna be on the next list to go to the infantry - as it turned out we weren't but they did send one more group. Some guys at the next table they were like headquarters people from the American Army and they had these lady guests and they was all dressed up, neckties and clothes all pressed and everything. Mason, Thompson and I - our clothes had what I called the "Barracks bag crease" - if you folded 'em up neatly when you put 'em away and put 'em in the bag then they would kinda stay halfway creased, but you'd end up with creases where you don't want em! I remember the singer of the band, he was singing "When my dreamboat comes home" but he didn't sing "boat", he sang "bowut". Under the influence I like to sing and have fun and I was about to challenge the man and get up there and sing a hill-billy song for him. I can't sing but when I'm drinking it don't make no difference, it all sounds good to me."

Chris Controwinski recalls that Frank Lechert had been the Truck Dispatcher ever since the desert, and..."when we got to Europe he was also responsible for the distribution of PX rations, cigarettes, soap, chocolate bars, toothpaste, and he did a fantastic job. They couldn't have found a better person, he couldn't have been more fair. By February 1945 Lechert was still a Corporal still doing the job, and soon after they discovered the job he was doing rated a Tech Sergeants stripes. For three years he had been dispatcher and keeping track of rations on the side. He finally got the stripes two or three months before we got out in 1945."

Fred Kennel had an interesting experience in Mons when he..."ran into American soldiers who had deserted from World War I and married Belgian girls. I often wonder, did their families know? does the government know? were they listed missing in action?"

The 146th didn't remain in Mons for too long but Fred Cox recalls..."we stayed in what was a private school, a Catholic convent or something then moved on. "

He also remembers..."a bunch of PoWs painting signs, painting "Passez Interdit", and the other was "Pas Fumez".

HEADQUARTERS

146TH QUARTERMASTER TRUCK COMPANY (TC)

U. S. ARMY

APO 228
1 February 1945

ROSTER - PERSONNEL

Capt.,QMC	BEASLEY Clifford M	0387310	1st Lt.,QMC	McMASTER William H	01575461
1st Lt.,QMC	VINCE Louis Jr		1st Lt.,QMC	KENYON Meril T	01703908
2nd Lt.,QMC	SINCLAIR Richard M	0536299			

1st Sgt	AXSELLE John F Jr	20348902	T/Sgt	CRANDALL John M	20348632
S/Sgt	AGNOR Marion D	33046747	S/Sgt	BELLO John J	20348653
S/Sgt	BRIENZA Louis J	20348631	S/Sgt	JOHNSON George E	33009257
S/Sgt	RUSSELL Reginald R Jr	20348647	Sgt	BAKER Linnie L	33042087
Sgt	FORNILL Frick	20348658	Sgt	HOLLETT John W	33009332
Sgt	LITTLE Francis E	20348783	Sgt	PERRY Robert D	33009330
Sgt	RHEA Aubrey A	33041704	Tec 4	CONTROWINSKI Chris	20348655
Tec 4	CRABTREE James P	33009214	Tec 4	KENNEL Fred E	20348643
Tec 4	MATHEWS Roland H	20348662	Tec 4	TEAGLE John W	20348667
Tec 4	WARD Paul P	20348794	Cpl	BECK Edward J	33050975
Cpl	BERRYMAN Lewis M	33042234	Cpl	CAHILL T L	33081008

Cpl	COOPER George M	33042068	Cpl	DENTON Bernard A	33042023
Cpl	DUNCAN Walter R	20348911	Cpl	FRAZER William D	33009164
Cpl	INMAN Clarance S	34143382	Cpl	LANG Alfred J	33009144
Cpl	LECHART Frank W Jr	33009120	Cpl	MASON Tonchie Y	33048805
Cpl	STUART Harry P	33009141	Cpl	WELLS Robert W	10610642
Cpl	WHITEMAN Marlin R	33017734			

Tec 5	AGNEW Victor D	36557529	Tec 5	ALDEN John J	20348650
Tec 5	ATKINS Carl J	33046565	Tec 5	BEACH Roscoe K	33009156
Tec 5	BEADLES Charles	20348905	Tec 5	BEADLES Leslie C	33042106
Tec 5	BEASLEY Raymond W	36525066	Tec 5	BERRY James H	33009370
Tec 5	BLUE Edward D	33009347	Tec 5	BRONNER Allen	33008799
Tec 5	BROWN James L	35753412	Tec 5	BRYANT James W Jr	20346471
Tec 5	BUDRES Leon J	32158539	Tec 5	BURNS Hermann L	35658448
Tec 5	CAMPBELL Lawrence	33635191	Tec 5	CAMPELLONE Furey	33778482
Tec 5	CARDER George O	35376458	Tec 5	CARROLL James	34494940
Tec 5	CARTER Lawrence P	36707669	Tec 5	CARTER Thomas E	34804407
Tec 5	CHAMBERS William H	34769332	Tec 5	CHEELEY Dennis W	33042227
Tec 5	COGHILL Garland P	20348957	Tec 5	COLLINS Spencer M	20348909
Tec 5	CORRAO Joseph	36656213	Tec 5	COX Frederick H	20348671
Tec 5	COX Jessie W	34142989	Tec 5	DAVIS Tilford A	38039255
Tec 5	DAVIS William	42024662	Tec 5	DIEHL William F	33574383
Tec 5	DI SANO Benjamin F	31148074	Tec 5	DISNEY William G	20348657
Tec 5	DOVYAK Frank B	33037021	Tec 5	DUGNAN Charles L	35601317
Tec 5	FISHER Emanuel	33042026	Tec 5	FORREST James W	34495588
Tec 5	FOSTER Lonnie S	34136684	Tec 5	GADOW Alfred	33009327
Tec 5	GEE Wilson W	33042212	Tec 5	HADSOCK Roscoe P	34530868
Tec 5	JENKINS Benedict E	33009382	Tec 5	KRIVZ Edward L	37285604
Tec 5	LAKER Charles M	33009265	Tec 5	LESTRANGE William F	33050995
Tec 5	LIGHT Robert A	33233829	Tec 5	LINCKS Virgil R	37106663
Tec 5	LONGANECKER Harry	35384355	Tec 5	LOUDERMELT Sylvest	34115151
Tec 5	MACKAY Clarence J	20348959	Tec 5	MORASCO Rosco J	32094265
Tec 5	OLIVER Stuart E	20349331	Tec 5	PACE Walter T	38230098
Tec 5	PARKER Henry M	34098313	Tec 5	POWELL Joel C	34576488
Tec 5	ROBERTSON Renso	34041167	Tec 5	SCOTT Solomon	33009103
Tec 5	SHAW Albert	20348665	Tec 5	STRUGALA Adam C	33055102
Tec 5	TAYLOR William	33042125	Tec 5	THIBEAULT Charles H	31077366
Tec 5	TOPPEL Elroy W Jr	20349338	Tec 5	VIRAG Paul	35551107
Tec 5	WALTER Stanley	33042167	Tec 5	WEBER Rudolph Jr	33081947
Tec 5	ZEMEL Michael	33009133			

Pvt 1cl	BUTCHER Cleo H	39248985	Pvt 1cl	OSOWSKI Edward E	31102612
Pvt 1cl	STONER Norvil H	13073135	Pvt 1cl	THIBODAUX George	34153513

Pvt	ANGSTADT Nathan	33077933	Pvt	BARKER Fred L	20348904
Pvt	BLAIR Archie B	18085425	Pvt	BONGO Michael	33151488
Pvt	CHESTHUNT Henry G	34804336	Pvt	COLE Lawrence O	32665896
Pvt	CRAWFORD Clifford K	14016580	Pvt	DESO James A	32664666
Pvt	FARLEY Hugh J	32709766	Pvt	GRIFFIN Paul P	6929175
Pvt	GRIMES Elbert	33450618	Pvt	HALK Michael M	32086875
Pvt	HAMILTON Charles R	33009362	Pvt	HOLT Henry R	13014950

Pvt	HORNSBY Charles	6986693		Pvt	HUCK Raymond A	37380402
Pvt	JANESKE Harry E	36149900		Pvt	KASTINA Joseph Jr	33009191
Pvt	LOCKRIDGE James M	6958147		Pvt	MOLLER George W	13136646
Pvt	MYERS George K	35592350		Pvt	PARKER Elijah G	37402259
Pvt	PRICE Emert	35446858		Pvt	PRIEST Gaylon R	33046629
Pvt	SHUTT Kirby J	19104321		Pvt	SWARTZLANDER Leroy	35550814
Pvt	VARNER Edd S	34143971		Pvt	WADDEL Thomas	35207680
Pvt	WARREN James S	34135700		Pvt	WARVIN Jessie A	20348672
Pvt	WERNER Livingston P	32810601		Pvt	WILSON Russell E	10675041

When the 146th made their first crossing of the Rhine, Fred Cox remembers..."We were stopped in Remagen waiting to go cross the bridge but either while we were waiting or just before we got there the bridge had collapsed, so we had to wait until a pontoon bridge was put together. It was after dark when we were finally able to cross that bridge. Now these pontoon bridges only had two treads going across the pontoon boats, they had a lip on the inner side to keep you from running off the edge. I had recently learnt from a guy who was in the Engineers that the lip was a four by four piece of timber and it had "C" clamps holding it onto the tread - that wasn't much of a lip for a truck. A big tyre could just run over it like a bicycle running over a cigarette butt. There was an aerial searchlight on each side of the bridge, each shining across to the opposite shore. Sergeant Russell was lining us up, waiting our turn to go on the bridge, when one truck got about the middle of the bridge he'd tell the next truck to start out. I don't know what he told the other guys but when I asked 'bout the lights he told me that he thought the Engineers thought German frogmen might try to blow the bridge so they had the searchlights there so they could spot 'em before they got all the way down to the bridge. So when it came to his turn to tell me to go he said "Keep in second gear so you don't go too fast" so I started getting near the middle - I started to ease down on the gas a little bit and I don't know if I was meant to do it or if it was a reflex action but unconsciously I just wanted to get off the damned thing. As soon as I started to pick up a little bit of speed the thing got to rockin', I lifted my foot up off the gas and it kept on rockin' I didn't know what the hell to do so I eased the gas down about half pedal and let her rock a little bit and gradually settle down, and I tell you I really thanked the Lord when I got off that thing."

Rudy Weber used that pontoon bridge several times..."the Rhine is very wide and has a very swift current - the Engineers must have had difficulty building the pontoon bridge. We crossed the Rhine many times with our semi-trailers loaded with supplies and for me each time was a hairy experience. The Army had sharpshooters posted about every four or six pontoons as the Germans would float explosives down the river trying to destroy or damage the bridge. As far as I know the sharpshooters did a good job."

Germany was becoming almost a blur to the 146th, just like France. The Allied advance had by now gathered such a rapid pace it was impossible to stay in any one place for more than a few days at a time if they were to keep up with the front line.

On one occasion Louis Brienza went to Essen..."it was levelled!"

Fred Kennel was..."moving through Germany one evening and trying to find a place to bivouac for a few days. Someone spotted a former concentration camp and we moved in to look it over. After spending a few hours debating on moving in, everyone started scratching. We all had to be deloused and we moved on to a patch of woods!"

Fred Cox remembers..."several convoys, and on one we hauled to the 104th Division called the "Timber Wolf" Division, had a wolf's head on the shoulder patch. I don't know what we hauled but on the way back I was hauling salvaged clothing, I was told it was clothing from dead and wounded. I was driving the lead truck and Sergeant Russell was riding with me, most of the other trucks were hauling German prisoners of war, they had about a hundred on each trailer with just one MP in the cab. They had the canvas top down on the cab and the MP rode with his back against the windshield so he'd be facing the prisoners, he had a "grease gun" with a little wire folding stock, so each MP was roughly was guarding a hundred prisoners. But I think after we'd bounced 'em through a few of them rougher roads they wouldn't have felt like running anyway! I think we took them back to Belgium."

Even while driving, Fred Cox was able to appreciate the architectural history of Germany..."I recall going through this walled town sat atop a low mountain, the streets were kinda windy and narrow, and I think the name was Marburg, it was rather quaint, early 1600s, and a novelty because everything was relatively new in the States."

Laing was a Company Clerk with, as John Axselle remembers..."a brilliant mind but come pay day he gonna get drunk. He'd go into town, get into trouble and the MPs bring him back. He'd had two or three court martials and I didn't want to lose him 'cause the guy, he had a script like the German print - beautiful, he was German. He had read the Bible and he could quote scriptures one end to the other. I made a deal with him, I said 'I'm gonna give you a rating of T5 and give you three days a month to get drunk and sober up, and I want you to take care of the payroll. He'd set up the payroll at night when everything was shut up, he'd get in the back of a truck, pull the sides down, with a gas lamp. Next morning he had that payroll ready to go. I said 'We'll get along fine' and do you know he did it. He was too valuable a person to lose. Intelligent conversation, well read, well educated, been in the Merchant Marine, but one of those souls never found his niche."

CHAPTER TWENTY SEVEN

Adendorf, Germany
1st - 5th April 1945

Bergheim, Germany
5th - 9th April 1945

Nechenheim, Germany
9th - 10th April 1945

Berkum, Germany
10th April - 25th May 1945

Duren, Germany
26th May - 15th June 1945

Munchen Gladbach, Germany
15th June - 1st July 1945

Halle, Germany
2nd - 6th July 1945

Berlin, Germany
6th July 1945 - 10th February 1946

7th May 1945:

Representatives of Nazi Germany's armed forces sign their unconditional surrender at General Eisenhower's Headquarters with military operations scheduled to end at 2301 hours the next day.

As the final stages of the U.S. offensive moved deeper into Germany, so did their supply dumps, some being over two hundred miles east of the Rhine. Replenished by truck convoys on ever lengthening journeys the vast distances involved brought problems of communication and control between units bivouacked along the entire length of the Main Supply Route.

Chris Controwinski has good reason to remember..."a place called Berkum, not far from Aachen, Cologne. At the time we had no idea where we were, we never saw any maps or anything, the roads were not marked. About that time they were looking for replacements for infantry divisions who had a lot of casualties as a result of the Battle of the Bulge and they said they wanted fifteen or twenty per cent of every service company to go back for infantry refresher training. They had these camps back in France and I was one of the lucky ones that got pulled out and sent back, I was gonna be cannon fodder after eight weeks and go up to an infantry division as a rifleman."

Fred Cox remembers him going..."we lost some guys and they put them in the infantry, fifteen of 'em, that's when we lost Gaylon Priest, we lost Chris Controwinski, we lost some other fellas too."

U.S. forces crossed the Elbe on the 12th April 1945, and Rudy Weber believes with the 146th he was on the first convoy across the river. Seeing Russians on the other side the drivers "put on a show" for them. They all engaged low gear then with one foot in the cab and holding onto the steering wheel with one hand, assumed a star position hanging out over the edge of the bridge away from their truck cabs. The Russians reaction is not remembered.

On the 4th of May 1945 the 146th QM Truck Company were operating under the 175th QM Battalion Mobile (Transportation Corps) who were in turn part of the 470th QM Group whose official history states they were..."relieved from assignment to the Transportation Section, ASCZ and moved to Schluchtern, Germany, 33 kilometres south of ASCZ located at Fulda, Germany with the mission of setting up and operating the ASCZ, Transportation Section Motor Pool. The following units were attached to the Group to handle commitments from Transportation Corps Section, ASCZ."

157th QM Bn Mobile (TC)	175th QM Bn Mobile (TC)	470th QM Bn Mobile (TC)
168th QM Truck Co (TC)	146th QM Truck Co (TC)	3396th QM Truck Co (TC)
3383rd QM Truck Co (TC)	3870th QM Truck Co (TC)	3397th QM Truck Co (TC)
3418th QM Truck Co (TC)	3985th QM Truck Co (TC)	3559th QM Truck Co (TC)
3625th QM Truck Co (TC)	4257th QM Truck Co (TC)	3619th QM Truck Co (TC)
3668th QM Truck Co (TC)	4260th QM Truck Co (TC)	4011st QM Truck Co (TC)
3681st QM Truck Co (TC)	4267th QM Truck Co (TC)	4259th QM Truck Co (TC)
3884th QM Truck Co (TC)		
4007th QM Truck Co (TC)		
4127th QM Truck Co (TC)		

"At present Battalions and Companies are scattered over a very wide area, both east and west of the Rhine River and operations are diversified more than at any time in this Group's history on the continent. Some Companies are hauling QM Classes I and III, others working on PWE, few for 15th Army and one handles the "Tout Sweet" run and seven companies are in what is called the ASCZ Pool that handle commitments coming from Transportation Corps Section, ASCZ."

Just before VE Day on 8th May 1945, the word was that the 146th were going to assist with the invasion of Japan as they were considered seasoned soldiers. It was also rumoured that they were to get new trucks and go to the 'Burma Road' - many threatened if they went to the Suez Canal again they'd all jump ship.

Duren, Germany had been taken by VII Corps of the U.S. 1st Army on February 25th and Fred Cox's arrival here was memorable..."man! that place was blowed up some kind of trouble, there was rubble piled about three stories high and just the roads ran through the rubble. We stayed in a maternity hospital for Hitler's unwed mothers who had been encouraged to have babies to build up the stock of the 'Master race'. The hospital had a wall round it and you had to go through a gate to get to it. The roof had been bombed onto the second floor and we lived down the first floor and there was a small building outside the back of it - the morgue."

While they were there, Fred Cox and all the others..."drew lots, two names on a paper in a hat and drew 'em out. Frank Dovyak and Virgil Links were the two lucky guys and they got a furlough back to England. Well they were gone seemed like a month. They went back to Bristol of course, and man I'd have given my left arm to be going back there but as it was I still got both my arms and never did get back to Bristol. Dovyak told me after he came back that when he walked into the Red Cross hotel to register, the first person he saw was Kay, my little English girl. She was now a volunteer helping the American Red Cross. Of course her first question was "How's Freddie?". Did my morale suffer a blow when he came back and told me that!

The area around Duren, so Fred Cox heard..."had been inundated by a ruptured dam. The water had now receded and bodies were being found and brought to the hospital morgue."

Elijah Parker came across a Canadian "Weasel" just like the ones that Fred Cox..."hauled to Maastricht, Holland. The thing had water in it and everything, water in the gas and oil, so after he'd baled it out and drained and replaced the oil and gasoline, got that thing going and drove it up to our Company area and drove it round like his own private vehicle. So Dovyak and I decided to go and see what we could scrounge up. We started walking across this small wood that had all this green fern growing there like a foot to a foot and a half high. I was slightly ahead of Dovyak and went to put my foot down and all of a sudden I see this rusty wire - it was a trip wire! Well I stepped over it and hollered to Frank so he wouldn't step on it and there was a daggone potato masher grenade settin' up about shin high eight to ten feet to the right of me. If the ferns hadn't been bright green and the wire rusty I might very well have ended my career with the Army, if not getting killed at least lost a leg."

A reunion was at the end of one detail for Fred Cox..."Near the end of May we got this job of hauling these trailers for this salvage company. It was a negro company and they would repair this clothing, they had sewing machines mounted on trailers and the sides would lift up and they could see out, have a lot of fresh air. We didn't haul the troops we only hauled their trailers. We towed them down to Marseilles, France and we went down beside the Rhone river and we had picked these trailers up near Dusseldorf, Germany. We went through Lyons and Dijon. We got down to Marseilles and we dropped off the trailers and we drove up to the Company area and met Lieutenant Albright! We stayed with them in Marseilles until we got ready to come back to Duren. Not having any weight on the back of the tractors them things rode really hard so we let half the air out of the rear tyres so it rode more comfortably. It was going to be about 750 miles we gonna be driving like this back to Duren. When we got back we found out that they had announced the Points System based on the amount of service, campaign stars, any medals you might have won, if you were married and had children - each child counted 12 points."

John Axselle remembers at Munchen Gladbach..."we picked up a bunch of Slavs. They were running away from the Nazis, and the Commies. They were like freedom fighters, and some of them were women - big rough mommas. They worked maintenance, changed tyres, in the kitchen and so forth. This was no official arrangement, it was just a pick-up deal - we came across PoWs and we kept 'em. They was doing good hard manual work and relieving guys doing fatigues - and they were happy, they were getting fed, had a nice warm place to sleep. And this slave labour, man they loved us, they thought we were God."

Rudy Weber remembers them too..."our German prisoners were taken from us and replaced with Polish refugees and slave labourers." And on arrival in any German town..."the first thing, you went to the Burgermeister and told him you needed billets for 'X' number of men. He in turn would clean out a block or so of civilians and we would move into their homes, they were allowed to work their gardens during daylight and we were friendly with these people, in fact around this time I got my T-5 rating but I had always said I would never sew any stripes on, so the lady of the house did it for me in exchange for some food. We didn't destroy anything but the home where the Polish Displaced Persons stayed was being trashed by them. Our officers, with me as interpreter put a stop to it fast. I told them if one more item was broken we would return them to the D.P. Compound. They were not about to give up three good meals a day and a roof over their heads."

The first meeting of the Inter-Allied Council for Berlin takes place on the 11th of July 1945 when the Soviets agree to turn over administration of the already allocated sectors of the city to the British and Americans who have already made their own arrangements to allocate some of their sectors to the French.

A few days later General Eisenhower announces the closure of SHAEF and eases some of the existing restrictions between American soldiers and German civilians.

President Truman has already approved plans for the invasion of Japan which require participation of American forces to be brought from Europe, but following the successful testing of the world's first atomic weapon in the New Mexico desert, it is approved to be used against Japan to try and shorten the war and obviate the necessity of mounting the invasion of Japan.

On the 8th of August 1945 the first atomic bomb is dropped on the Japanese city of Hiroshima and the following day, another on Nagasaki.

To the complete and utter surprise of the Japanese civilian population who have only been fed propaganda news, the nation surrenders on the 15th of August, issuing a cease fire order to all its forces the following day and signing the documents of surrender aboard the battleship USS *Missouri* anchored in Tokyo Bay on the 2nd of September 1945.

The western world has realised through the experiences of the Second World War that conflict on such a scale must never ever happen again and in an attempt to unite the nations of the world in that common purpose the United Nations organisation was born.

Their Charter comes into force on the 24th of October with a creditable twenty nine signatories, but during the very first meetings in London there are violent disagreements between the Soviets and their former Western allies, heralding decades of uneasy peace between East and West

During May, June and July 1945, Rudy Weber recalls the 146th..."supplied our Berlin garrison. The railroad went as far as Helmstedt, about one mile from the Russian zone in the British sector. It was about a hundred miles from Helmstedt to Berlin and at first we were told not to object if the Russians took things off our trucks. After a time we ran with an armoured car in front and rear of our convoys - no more problems!"

Around July 1945 Jim Brown remembers..."most of the 146th left. There was still Jo Corrao, myself, Chuck Duignan, Bill Davis, Dick Sinclair - he was the Commanding Officer from Christmas 1945 until early 1946. I don't know how many Americans there were, not many because all the rest were Japanese-Americans. They were replacements and we stayed with them because we didn't have enough points yet to come home."

So he..."ran convoys from Berlin to Paris, and I'd take one platoon at a time, then they'd come back and then take another platoon, and I was doing all this as a Corporal! We went to Paris and we'd park the trucks in a Motor Pool with an M.P. and a guard and a fence around it - and we'd take off for three or four days - just have a good time. But we always ended up at the Moulin Rouge. We had black market money and we could live it up. Walter Pace loved to play cards and he would never go on a convoy, just sit around and play cards all the time, and every time I went in he'd be playing cards, and I'd say 'what you want me to bring you back?' He'd say 'Bring back some wine or potatoes, or bread or something'. Well we kept a lot of people from starving in Berlin and he'd throw me whatever his winnings were, maybe three or four thousand dollars, we'd go to town and on the way back stop and buy the food. We took back French bread, potatoes, almost anything and we'd go to families and distribute it. Now these semi-trailers had a box on the side of 'em, supposed to be for tarps to fit in - they would hold an awful lot of food. We were never checked, we had no problems, we were the only ones on the road. Then they came up with this Checkpoint 'Charlie' but they didn't check the trucks - more aggravation than anything else."

Jim Brown stayed in Berlin long enough to take charge of German truck drivers at Templehof airport when the Berlin Airlift began, but by now the 146th had passed into glorious history.

CHAPTER TWENTY EIGHT

GOING HOME

Berger Bankston was probably the first of the original Company 'A' members to return to the United States..."In Tripoli I had ear trouble, I went to the Medics and they flew me back to Cairo for treatment, then they flew me back to Tripoli, I rejoined the Company and later on they flew me back to Cairo again and this time I went before a board who determined that I should go back to the States. At this point I left the 146th. On the convoy from Port Said to Gibraltar we saw a German submarine sunk by our convoy and we were in an extremely bad storm, one of the worst storms at sea that I've ever seen. We were in a rather close formation convoy going through the Mediterranean, and when we woke up the next morning the ship that was behind us was missing. The rumour was that the ship had capsized during the night and everybody on board was lost. At Greenock, Scotland I boarded a train for Kidderminster and the 52nd General Hospital, on the way they had an air raid so they stopped our hospital train inside a tunnel. I thought that was a crazy thing to do, the bombs hit that tunnel and seal us in there we'd never get out!

After treatment Berger Bankston was..."re-assigned to Camp Lee, Virginia while the Company was still over in Europe. Lieutenant Walston was quite famous at Camp Lee, everyone having to do with the truck driving school there knew about him, and when they found out I had come from his company I was looked up to as being somebody who knew what I was talking about when it came to trucks and convoys. I was assigned as an instructor there to teach truck drivers, that was my first assignment when I came back. "Bull Moose" used to tell those fellas wild stories about the 146th in Africa, most of the people he was training were apparently black troops. He went overseas a second time with a black company and he was telling them stories that the 146th was shooting down Me109s from the ground with .30 calibre rifle fire and stories of that type. When some of our boys later on ran into those black troops in England they knew who the 146th was from Lieutenant Walston and repeated some of those stories that he had told them and they thought the 146th was quite famous and our boys revelled in the glory."

Chris Controwinski, although separated from the 146th as a replacement infantryman met up with some of his friends sooner than he expected..."I was in Compiegne, France when Roosevelt died, and on VE Day, 8th May 1945 I had about two more weeks to go on that basic training before I was gonna go to an infantry division as a rifleman. Then they came out with the points system and I had about 115 points and here I am with these guys from other outfits that hadn't been over very long - some were fresh over from the States taking this refresher - and I got assigned to guard duty at one of these staging camps where they started setting the guys up to send them home. If you were married and had been in combat and you had 89 points you had 'priority one' to go home. And I'm doing guard duty, me and a couple of other guys left over from the 146th - we survived Compiegne and were in a place called Royal Lieu with a staging area beside the road. These guys were coming back from combat divisions and I respected them, I didn't complain, they're coming back with 89, 92 points and going home, and they talked to us while we were doing guard duty to stop them from goofing off, from looking for women and beer so they don't miss their call to go home, and they'd say "How many points you got?" and I'd say "I got 115" and they'd either call us a damn liar or a damn fool and then "You're crazy, you're over here doing guard duty!" "Yea but I don't mind, I didn't get to go up to the front I missed it and thank God I'm alive".

"It finally came to be our turn and me and a couple of other guys, one guy in particular, Jimmy Bryant - he and I stayed together to the very end. We left the Royal Lieu staging area, we rode those damned forty and eight cars, almost froze to death, we went back through Compiegne and he remembered a bar there and the train stopped for a while and he ran to this bar, he knew the women that ran it and he came back with a bottle of cognac and that kept us from freezing to death. I think we went to Amsterdam and finally got assigned to a liberty ship to come home. They only had so many billets on the ship and they counted so many men to go home and we were near the tail end of it, and we had no outfit, we were almost itinerant troops, eligible to go home but Privates and they put us where they could find a spot. Well they filled up this liberty ship and they had ten or fifteen of us left over and they said 'well you've got two choices, you can wait for the next ship or you can go on this one and hope you can find somebody to hot bunk with' In other words when they were out of the bunk during the day you could sleep during the day but you had to be there meal times, and we said 'Hell we've been over here long enough we'll take our chances hot bunking' - and we sorta lost. We did get home in about ten days, but it was a rough trip with a lot of seasick people, there were no bunks available during the day because it was rough weather and most of them wanted their bunks. So we slept on the decks or on tables in the mess hall wherever we could find a place to lay down, but I survived that and we got back to Hampton Roads, Virginia. Put us on a train, we came back up through Washington and back out to Fort Meade which is where I got my discharge somewhere around July 1945. The rest of the Company stayed together as the 146th, they didn't all come home together they came home in fives and tens and twenties, the 146th as we knew it were back home by July 1945."

Surely nobody had such bad luck as Rudy Weber..."By this time us older men had many more points than were needed for rotation home so we were split into three groups. The first left in early June by air, the second group left in early July by air. I was in the third group with 103 points, and was transferred to another unit from early July to early August until I flew from Berlin to France. I was waiting for air transport home when Japan surrendered and all air transport was cancelled. They held a boat at Cherbourg the two days it took to change our travel orders from air to sea and on 20th August 1945 sailed in a Liberty ship arriving in New York on 3rd September. During the voyage half the men slept below and the other half slept on deck and the two groups were supposed to swop every day. I found a man who wished to stay on deck so we didn't move every day. We also ran into a storm that lasted three days and all the ship could do was head into the wind."

"After landing in New York we went to Fort Dix, New Jersey for the night and I had my first fresh milk in three years. Next we went to Indiantown Gap, Pennsylvania and I was discharged on 7th September 1945, 75 miles and a two hour bus trip from home."

John Crandall arrived back in the States on 1st July 1945 and was honourably discharged six days later at Fort Meade in the rank of Technical Sergeant, re-enlisting in the Headquarters Detachment of the D.C. National Guard just over a year later and finally leaving on 3rd August 1950 as a Master Sergeant after almost continuous service to the National Guard since October 1926.

When John Axselle left for home..."I left a P.38 and a Luger there, bin told you couldn't carry a firearm home on board ship which turned out to be hokum. They said we gonna have a shakedown inspection but nobody shook anybody down. We stopped in Versailles for about two weeks and I gained weight like crazy, we had German prisoners waiting on you like maid service. They changed your German money to American money, weighed your luggage and I never saw 'em look in a bag."

"They flew us down to Casablanca to a 'reple depot' and each unit had a number. There was eight in my group and we were assigned to a squad tent. All night and all day they say 'Group so and so report to the centre' and if you didn't show up in a period of time, you missed the plane, then you have to wait your turn and come all the way round again. When a plane became available they'd call a group. The lights stayed on just like a big PoW compound, wire round it - all you did was shoot crap, play cards and get chow."

"They called our number 'bout midnight, put us on a truck that carried us out to a DC54. We left there and flew all night to Dakar. Some were asleep, some were reading and some were playing cards on a life raft in the middle of the aircraft. The co-pilot came back and joined the card game, wasn't long before the pilot came back. Someone looked up and said 'Hey! who's flying the plane?'. But that was the neatest thing that automatic pilot."

"We ate breakfast in Dakar, took off for South America and landed at Natel where they used to ferry the bombers across. We flew on that night, stopped at British Guyana, ate something, had breakfast in Puerto Rico, next stop Miami, Florida. We got in about 1 or 2 o'clock in the afternoon and it was the most beautiful sight I ever saw in my life, all those lights at night, couldn't believe it was real."

"We stopped for about a week in squad tents among palm trees and sand! Then they made up a train and wherever you were mustered into Federal service, they made up a car, and they started down in Georgia. They cut this car off, South Carolina cut off a car, North Carolina, Virginia and then Maryland - thats where they cut us off, they were going all the way up to New York. They just cut the car off and let us sit until a bus picked us up and took us to Fort Meade. For a week or ten days we had examinations and this that and the other, but do you know the most lonesome feeling of my life - who am I? Was the day they lined us up and a guy gets up and read a little speech about Congress and the President of the United States thank you for your service, you are now discharged from the service of the United States Army. You don't have a home, you had a home but you don't have a home. Everything that you were an integral part of, everything that was you has gone."

"I had without a doubt one of the most wonderful families that God ever let live - and they tolerated me. But I was the most miserable, unhappy person. I didn't speak their language - I was profane and my family had never been profane. Everything was J.C., S.o.B., and they would cringe, but that to me was communication. I'd play crap or play poker - all those bad habits - I was like a fish out of water. It took a while to settle down, I was at home in the military, I felt like a stranger at home in my own home, I felt like I didn't belong there - I belonged with the outfit."

Garland Coghill went home..."as one of the first on account of points and I went to Le Havre, France and boarded a Liberty ship for home."

Fred Cox was in Duren when..."we found out that they had announced the Points system. Each month of service in the States counted 1 point, each month overseas counted 2 points, each battle star counted 5. They told us if you had 103 or more you on the first list to come home. Man I tried to count my points up real quick and I finally figured I had 108, whoopee! I was gonna be going home! and sure enough a few days later we were hauled to a train, and can you imagine us truck drivers riding in a forty and eight boxcar. We had a little bit of straw to sit on, all the people we hauled, all the stuff we hauled, now we gonna be discharged and we gotta ride in a boxcar. What in the First World War they called a forty and eight - 40 men and 8 mules!" As each man boarded the train they were handed a single sheet of paper.

OFFICE OF THE TRAIN COMMANDER
Somewhere in Germany
* * *

SUBJECT   :Instructions to be observed while aboard this train
TO   :Each Officer and Enlisted Man

1.   So you're going home, Soldier! Let's get there safely and in an orderly manner. Your cooperation in the following points will make it quite simple:

  a.   Do not discuss this move with unauthorised persons
  b.   Do not detrain without orders.
  c.   Do not throw rubbish out of windows.
  d.   Do not lean out of windows.
  e.   Do not damage railway or Government property.
  f.   Do not mark or write anything on sides of cars.
  g.   Do not use gasoline cookers.
  h.   Do not waste water in lavatories.
  i.   Do not ride anywhere on train except where authorized.

2.   The officer or NCO in charge of your car is your temporary commander. His word is law. Should you become ill or injured enroute, he will conduct you to the First Aid Station aboard the train.
Most of your meals will be K-Rations. Place all trash in receptacles provided in cars for same and keep your car clean at all times.
Everything that _can_ be furnished you on this train has been provided. Remember the other fellow and he will remember you.

3.   The following time schedule is furnished for your information:

Leave Gotzenhof	06 1600 June
Arrive Hanau	06 2125 June
Depart Hanau	06 2155 June
Arrive Gau Angesheim	07 0300 June
Arrive Bad Godesburg	07 0900 June (Water-Latrine)
Depart Bad Godesburg	07 1100 June
Arrive Liege	07 1900 June (Water-Latrine)
Depart Liege	07 2100 June
Arrive Aulnoy	08 0600 June
Arrive St Quentin	08 0930 June (Water-Latrine)
Depart St Quentin	08 1130 June
Arrive Tergnier	08 1230 June
Arrive Compiegne	08 1530 June

4.   Yours for a safe trip home, Soldier, after a swell job done. God Bless you and yours.

JEFFERSON E. KIDD
Colonel, AGD
Train Commander.

It was tedious and boring on that train and time meant little to Fred Cox..."I don't remember how long we rode on the train but we went to Compiegne, France and while we were there one of the first people we see when we get there's Chris Controwinski! He's working guard duty. He went from us when we first got to Germany and sent to the infantry and they sent him back to France to train which was nice, he didn't get to any action in the infantry. He was guard there and he had the same amount of points that we did roughly so he should have bin comin' home with us, instead he was stuck in another outfit there and he was having to stay."

"They give us physicals and we turned in excess clothing. What they did, they made us strip down, put all our clothes except our shoes and under draws and raincoat, we put our shoes and raincoat on and everything else put in a duffle bag and carried with us to get our physical and put 'em back on and take our duffle bag out in a field and they started unloading the duffle bag, took a half pace away and they started telling us what we could have, and once we got all that there then we had to step away from whatever's left. That's how they separated us from our "extras", equipment we weren't supposed to have, so any little goodies you may have scavenged you had to leave. I had an Italian Beretta 6.25 mm that I had from when I was in the desert, and I had a paper that proved it was a trophy so they didn't take that from me. Now we went to another camp from Compiegne, it was just a tent camp and very crude, we only stayed there a day or two then we went to a camp called "Herbert Tareyton" named after another brand of cigarette, and it was near Le Havre. The only thing I can remember about that was we exchanged our French money for American money, then in a day or two we got on a boat, a Liberty ship called the ss *Caleb Strong* and so we headed for home."

"It took us fifteen days and we landed in Norfolk, Virginia on July 1st 1945, it was a Sunday about 2 pm. There were two or three officers and five or six enlisted Womens Army Corps, and the WACs were driving the trucks that hauled us from the dock to the camp. They hauled us to Camp Patrick Henry, we got there about supper time, four or five o'clock, so then they said that you can call home but the operators would take a certain time to put 'em through so you had to put your name in and the phone number you wanted then you had to hang around, wait for the operator to place the call. So as a line got open then she would announce over a loudspeaker go to such and such a number telephone. Well about nine o'clock that night I was able to get a phone call through to home. My brother Charles answered the phone he had just gotten home after three years on Ascension Island and in the Belgian Congo, so this was quite a pleasant surprise for him to answer the phone."

"After a day or two we rode a train to Fort Meade, arriving at night as usual - seemed like everything I did was night time. But anyway after being processed and having a physical and so forth we were discharged at approximately 5 pm July 8th 1945 - Amen brother!"

Looking back, John Axselle believes he was able to cope because..."You take an infantryman - they more or less tied down to one spot. The thing that helped me through the whole war was the fact that, hell we're not gonna be here for so long before I'm gonna be seeing something different. This is tough but things'll get better, there's gotta be a town up ahead where we can get some booze and some broads!"

Christmas 1945, John Axselle heard from the 'old' British seaman he met on the ss *Otranto*..."You and I, your folk, my folk at this time of the year, realise what this seasonal greeting means, what memories they recall. So here's your Rebel Brother sending you a few lines to let you know that I'm still with you and trust you and the remainder of the 'Gang' are well. Keep your eye on the target John and please pass a Cheerio to all the others."

Freddie Cox

When Fred Kennel got home he heard from two of his desert acquaintances. One letter was from his 51st Highlander 'deserter' from Benghazi, the other was from 'Bill' - " How do you like being in civvy street? or would you rather be in the sand and Tripoli - Good Old Days! I went to France on D Day and stayed on 'til ten days before the finish. I haven't been back since and I'm not sorry. Lets hope Fred if we ever meet again its in different circumstances, and if you ever come to England always remember the door will be wide open for you and the family, walk right in don't knock ..."

Jock's letter to Fred Kennel read..."yours truly is still in the army. I'm stationed in Italy at the present moment, but I expect to be going out of the army shortly. That little bit of trouble that I was in when I met you was straightened out. I wasn't even charged for it. The medical officers said I was suffering from minor shell shock and that I was no use for further service in the front line. The result was I got away scot free without a stain on my record. I'm damned glad the war is over now Freddie, for all our sakes. It was pretty rotten while it lasted wasn't it. It's up to us to make sure that there is never another one."

As the din of battle died down the American nation felt the same responsibility as Jock.

Through adversity they had blossomed into a world super-power with the ability to exert a stabilising influence around the globe, and they had also learned their lesson of 1941, vowing never again to allow their armed forces to plummet to such inadequate and ill-prepared depths.

The recruitment of a peace-time army was therefore of the highest priority and many War Department publications of the day took advantage of wartime achievements and victories to encourage the enlistment of would be men-at-arms.

Quartermaster Truck Companies were no exception, explaining their role in the post-war army through the publication of an illustrated, explanatory booklet it could have been written with the 146th in mind.

MISSION:

Quartermaster truck companies provide motor transportation for army personnel and supplies. In all areas of a theater of operations, from the ports of debarkation to the fighting fronts, quartermaster trucks haul troops, prisoners, food, gasoline, animals, weapons - in fact, anything that must be transported from Ammunition to Zippers.

ORGANISATION AND PERSONNEL:

Quartermaster truck companies are of two types. The "light" truck company (five officers and 105 enlisted men) is equipped with two and one-half-ton trucks and is designated either as a quartermaster truck company (when its primary mission is hauling cargo) or as a quartermaster troop transport company (when its primary mission is hauling personnel). The "heavy" truck company (five officers and 112 enlisted men) is equipped with big tractor-trailers and is designated as either a quartermaster truck company (heavy), when its primary mission is hauling cargo, or as a quartermaster truck company (petroleum), when it is equipped with tank semi-trailers for hauling bulk petroleum products. Both companies are composed of a company headquarters and three platoons. The company headquarters, in addition to normal administrative functions, has control of the trucking operations and operates the maintenance shop for the company. Each platoon may operate either as part of the company or as a separate unit if the situation demands. When a truck company is regularly operating twenty-four hours a day, additional drivers are authorized so that two-shift operation is possible.

TRAINING:

Every member of a quartermaster truck company must be a well-trained soldier as well as a specialist. Since the trucks, operating either singly or in convoy, are common targets for air and mechanized attack, drivers must be able to defend themselves and their loads. Driving over every kind of road, in darkness and daylight, in fair weather and foul, under threat of enemy attack near the front or in city traffic in the communications zone, the "truck jockeys" must operate their vehicles skilfully to keep them rolling. Maintenance must be constant and thorough so that the trucks can perform their mission. Personnel of the quartermaster truck companies receive instruction in all of these subjects in the course of their military and technical training. The final step in the training of a company is a period of team training during which the individuals learn to perform their mission as members of an integrated team.

OPERATIONS OF THE COMPANY:

Quartermaster truck companies are assigned to higher headquarters such as theaters of operations, communications zones, armies, separate corps, and task forces. Three to six companies assigned to a given headquarters are then attached to a quartermaster battalion headquarters and dispatched as requested. For example, six truck companies together with organic transportation can motorize an infantry division, or several companies can haul supplies from ships to storage areas. Generally, requests for transportation by an installation or organization come to the battalion headquarters, which in turn designates the companies to dispatch the vehicles needed.

Truck companies operate in all areas of a theater of operations. In the communications zone, trucks are used to supplement rail transportation. In combat zones, trucks are used almost exclusively, because rail transportation may be disrupted by enemy action. Over one-third of the truck companies in the European Theater operated in the combat zone.

SERVICE RENDERED:

Trucking isn't glamorous - rather it consists of a series of gruelling assignments, hauling anything and everything wherever it must go. Quartermaster truckers spanned the sandy desolation of the Sahara and nosed up the tortuous ascents from the blistering heat of the Persian Gulf to the shivering temperatures of the Iranian mountains. They inched their way through the treacherous passes of the Appenines and the Himalayas and skidded through the jungles of the Pacific islands. They highballed the Red Ball Express up a one-way lane to the German Reich itself and hauled the supplies of the armies that converged on Berlin. The drivers often operated twenty-four hours a day, sleeping in their trucks and eating cold C rations for days on end. They earned the respect of the combat troops and caused one American general to say, "The two and one-half ton truck is our most valuable weapon."

BATTLE IMPORTANCE:

Quartermaster truck companies made victory possible. The supplies and the troops delivered by their vehicles made it possible for our armies to complete their mission.

Over forty-five truck companies were awarded the invasion arrowhead for participating in amphibious landings. Truck companies of the Fifth Army, in addition to their other hauling, delivered 1,500 tons of food, 1,800 tons of gasoline, and fifty tons of clothing daily. A heavy truck company delivered 27,000,000 gallons of gasoline to the Seventh Army in thirty-eight days.

During the "Battle of the Bulge", another company operated continuously for thirty-six hours in moving troops and barely escaped as the Germans broke through. From November, 1944 to February, 1945, truck companies of the Ninth Army hauled 300,000 tons of supplies and 200,000 troops while driving 2,500,000 miles. Twenty thousand drivers of 174 truck companies delivered 200,000 tons of supplies from Cherbourg to the lines beyond Paris during the twenty-six-day life of the Red Ball Express.

Bill Albright is the only surviving officer of the 146th QM Truck Company to be traced, and it is his firm belief that credit for the 146th performing their duties with such pride, dedication and professionalism is almost entirely due to the quality and continuity of its non-commissioned officers.

As with any army, the non-commissioned officers run the outfits, but Bill Albright goes further..."When you think of it, as far as the Platoon Sergeants were concerned, Louis Brienza was Platoon Sergeant throughout the entire history of the 146th. Reggie Russell was the same, and then George Johnson took John Axselle's place, and he was with us full time. That continuity of non-commissioned officers ran the Company. Officers passed through - I was there for a while, then I was with the 404th, then I got re-connected in England, did one Red Ball convoy and they had me off in another Truck Company."

First Sergeant John Axselle's view is that..."The heart and guts and soul of the military is non-commissioned officers. They are the daddies and the troops are the kids."

His reflection on..."The guys of the outfit? I guess you could say we were the least disciplined in many respects than most any outfit in the Army, but I had a working relationship with the non-coms and I certainly respected the officers and they respected me, and the point was do your job - do your duty, forget all the frivolities and bull crap, just get the job done and do it damned good, and then if you want to - raise a little hell. Thats fine but don't let it interfere with what you have to do. And we got along great."

"THE TOBACCO CHEWING, TIRE KICKING BLUES"

When the roll is called "up yonder",
And St. Peter gives us our grade,
There are some who will cry and whimper,
And try to make a trade,
But the ones who will stand the tallest,
Without a murmur - a cry - or a kick,
Are the tobacco chewing, tire kicking bastards,
Of the One Hundred Forty Six.

We helped chase Rommel out of Africa,
And rolled across Flanders Fields,
We hauled the bombs and the petrol,
And dead bodies from the Channel's yield,
We did it all with Old Glory waving,
Without a murmur - a cry - or a kick,
The tobacco chewing, tire kicking bastards,
Of the One Hundred Forty Six.

Every year we all get together,
To tell war stories and share past events,
We try to relive those moments,
With nostalgia that won't relent,
We do it without shame for the tear in our eye,
Nor a murmur - a whine - or a kick,
The tobacco chewing, tire kicking bastards,
Of the One Hundred Forty Six.

Berger Bankston

APPENDICES

APPENDIX A

Company 'A'
104th QUARTERMASTER
REGIMENT
(1938)

Lt Stanley E. Travers

1st Sgt Donald S. Funk *

SERGEANTS:

Hubert L Cocke	Norman L Holst*	Martin R. Keough*
John M Crandall	Warren Hughes*	John N. Kailor*
George H Harper*		

CORPORALS:

Louis J Brienza*	Cecil R Sumner	John Wenn*
Nicholas Sparacino	William H Woodend*	

PRIVATES FIRST CLASS:

Anthony Brienza*	Norman W Hager*	Clarence A Phelps*
John L Cox	Arthur T Johnston*	Pierce A Sykes
Syanley Dennison	Harlow W Kiblinger	Phillip N Wagoner
Paul A Grolock*	William T Meany*	John C Wilson

PRIVATES:

Sidney Blanken	Alphonse S. Howes	Elmer L. Rollins
John A. Booker	Julian M. Johnston*	Edward E. Rozga
Robert L. Brillante	John C. Leon	Robert M. Schaefer
De Marr A. Canter	Chester A. Megill	Golden Smith
James F. Doerner	Ethelbert Miller	William P. Smith
Pasquale D. Del Grosso	Barney V. Moose*	Eugene E. Sumpter
Michael Fattibene	Billy B. Pennington	Charles E. Turner
John W. Goodwin	Edward M. Perkins	John E. White
Raymond E. Haliday	William C. Phelps	Sol Zipkin
Walter R. Harry	Samuel M. Pullman	

* = members of company A on date of muster 26/5/1936

Company 'A'
104th QUARTERMASTER
REGIMENT
(1940)

FIRST BATTALION

Major Fletcher F. Bernsdorff

1st Lt William D. Putnam	Cpt Henry B. Cockrell	1st Lt Henry M. Boudinot
Headquarters	Company 'A'	Company 'B'

| 2nd Lt Stanley W. Phillips | 1st Lt Stanley E. Travis | 1st Sgt Martin R. Keough * |

SERGEANTS:

Louis J Brienza*	John M Crandall	George H Harper*
Hubert L Cocke	Merrit H Gale	John N Kailor*
Nicholas Sparacino		

CORPORALS:

DeMarr A Canter	Cecil R Sumner	Louis B Toth
Chester A Megill	William H Woodend*	

PRIVATES FIRST CLASS:

Paul G Bassette	John A Looney	Edward E Rozga
Robert L Brillante	Clarence A Phelps*	Golden Smith
Michael Fattibene	Robert B Royal	Charles E Turner

PRIVATES:

Robert Byers	Harlow W Kiblinger	Philip H Proctor
Homer L Bryan	Rufus K King	Samuel L Pullman
Jack Chapman Joseph L Kunkle	Caroll B Rumbaugh	John L Cox
John W McKay	Robert M Schaefer	William R Fisher
Eugene M McLemore	William P Smith	John H Goodwin
Virgil E Manuel	Eugene E Sumpter	Leonard A Greenwald
Carl F H Milch	Harry Tucker	George W Hutton
William C Phelps	George S Wagerman	Jesse A Warvin

* = members of company A on date of muster 26/5/1936

APPENDIX B

146TH QM TRUCK COMPANY PERSONNEL

Notes:
[1] - listed in veterans booklet (issued to 146th members in Germany)
A,B,C,D - original Company 104th Quartermaster Regiment

	State of Origin	Service Number	Rank last known	Unit on discharge	Notes
ABRAMS Seymour L		33051013	Private First Class		
ALBRIGHT William R		01573003	1st Lieutenant	4268 QMTr Co	(146th First Lieutenant)
AGNOR Marion D	Virginia	3046747	Tech Sergeant	4260 QM Tr Co	[1] (146th Staff Sergeant)
AGNEW Victor D	Michigan	36557529	Technician 5		deceased
ALDEN John J	Dist Columbia	20348650	Technician 5		A [1] deceased
ALEXANDER Allen L	Washington				[1]
ANDERSON Carl E	New York	32731240	Private		
ANGSTADT Nathan W		33077933	Technician 5		
ATKINS Carl J	Virginia	33046565	Technician 4	146 QM Tr Co	[1] deceased
AXSELLE John F Jr	Virginia	20348902	First Sergeant	4207 QM Tr Co	C [1] (146th First Sergeant)
BABBIS Nicholas		20348651	Sergeant		A
BAKER Linnie L	Virginia	33042067	Sergeant	146 QM Tr Co	[1] deceased
BALDUCCI Paul	Mississippi				[1]
BANKSTON Berger M	Maryland	20348658	Sergeant		A (146th Corporal)
BARKER Fred L	Virginia	20348904	Technician 5	4260 QM Tr Co	[1] (146th PFC) deceased
BARLOW Greero	Mississippi				[1]
BASS Stanley	Illinois				
BEACH Roscoe K	Maryland	33009156	Technician 5	146 QM Tr Co	[1]
BEADLES Charles	Virginia	20348905	Technician 5	4260 QM Tr Co	[1] (146th T5) deceased
BEADLES Leslie C	Virginia	33042106	Technician 5	4260 QM Tr Co	[1] (146th Corporal)
BEARSCOVE Karl	Washington				A
BEASLEY Clifford M	Maryland	0-387310	Captain		[1] (146th 1st Lt) deceased
BEASLEY Raymond W	Michigan	36525066	Technician 5		[1]
BECHTEL Ambrose C	Ohio				
BECK Edward J	New Jersey	33050975	Corporal		[1] "Barrel"
BECKWITH Clifford	New York				
BELLO John J	Dist Columbia	20348653	Staff Sergeant	146 QM Tr Co	A [1] deceased
BENNETT Robert L		33042098	Corporal		deceased
BERCIK Michael P	Pennsylvania				[1]
BERRY James H	Maryland	33009370	Technician 5	4260 QM Tr Co	A [1] (146th T5)
BERRYMAN Lewis M	Virginia	33042234	Corporal	146 QM Tr Co	A [1]
BIANCHINI Andrew	Rhode Island				
BIEDRZYCKI Henry A		33051017	Private		deceased
BLAIR Archie B	Oklahoma	18085425	Private		[1]
BLUE Edward O	Virginia	33009347	Technician 5	4260 QM Tr Co	[1] (146th PFC and T5)
BOEGER Alfred A	New York				[1]
BOHNKER Eugene W	Iowa				[1]
BONGO Michael	Pennsylvania	33151488	Private		
BOWLES Alvin					A not overseas
BOWLES John					A not overseas
BOYD Earl	Tennessee				[1]
BREWER Bailey H	Alabama				
BRIENZA Louis J	Dist Columbia	20348631	Staff Sergeant	146 QM Tr Co	A [1]
BRONNER Allen	Maryland	33008799	Technician 5	4260 QM Tr Co	[1] joined in Middle East deceased
BROUGHT Calvin H		0-1575791	2nd Lieutenant		
BROWN Earl W	West Virginia				[1]
BROWN James L	West Virginia	35753412	Technician 5		[1] joined in Middle East (146th Cpl)
BRUNINGHAUS Vincent A	New York				[1]
BRYANT James W Jr		20346471	Technician 5		deceased
BUDRES Leon J	New Jersey	32158539	Technician 5	4260 QM Tr Co	[1] (146th T5)
BURNS Hermann L	West Virginia	35658448	Technician 5		[1] (146th Pvt)
BUTCHER Cleo H	Texas	39248985	Private First Class		[1]
BUZINE Charles D		33051027	Private		

CAHILL Thomas L	Pennsylvania	33081008	Corporal		'
CALLAHAN Raymond J	Maine				
CAMPBELL Lawrence W	West Virginia	33635191	Technician 5		'
CAMPELLONE Furey A	Pennsylvania	33778482	Technician 5		'
CARDER George O	West Virginia	35376458	Technician 5		'
CARROLL James	Tennessee	34494940	Technician 5		'
CARTER Lawrence P	Illinois	36707669	Technician 5		'
CARTER Paul E	Indiana				'
CARTER Thomas E	Alabama	34804407	Technician 5		'
CHAMBERS William H	Georgia	34769332	Technician 5		'
CHANATSKY Nathan	New Jersey				'
CHANDLER Andrew J	N Carolina				
CHANEY Theodore W		33042056	Private		died in Palestine
CHAPLIK Harry W	Pennsylvania				
CHEELEY Dennis W	Virginia	33042227	Technician 5	4267 QM Tr Co	' (146th T5)
CHESTNUT Henery G Jr	Alabama	34804336			' (146th Pvt)
COCKRELL Henry B			Captain		A not overseas
COGHILL Garland P	Virginia	20348957	Technician 5	146 QM Tr Co	'
COLE Lawrence O	New York	32665896	Private		
COLEMAN John M Jr		33041822	Corporal		
COLLINS Spencer M	Virginia	20348909	Technician 5	146 QM Tr Co	' joined in Middle East
COMMARATA John		32911090	Private		
CONTROWINSKI Chris S	Dist Columbia	20348655	Technician 4		A
CONWAY Leo F		33051011	Sergeant		
COOK Herschel C	Missouri				'
COOLEY Ivan E	Michigan				'
COOPER George M	Virginia	33042068	Corporal	4259 QM Tr Co	' (146th T5) deceased
CORRAO Joseph	Illinois	36656213	Technician 5	146th QM Tr Co	' joined in Europe
COURTNEY Sylvester R	Kansas				'
COX Frederick H	Maryland	20348671	Technician 5	146 QM Tr Co	A ' deceased
COX Jessie W	Tennessee	34142989	Technician 5		
COX John L		20348635	Sergeant		A deceased "Lester"
CRABTREE James P	Maryland	33009214	Technician 4	4260 QM Tr Co	' (146th T5) deceased
CRABTREE Paul P			Technician 5		deceased 2d Platoon
CRANDALL John M	Maryland	20348632	Technician Sgt	146 QM Tr Co	A '
CRAWFORD Clifford K		14016580	Private		
CROCE Robert E		33041542	Private First Class		deceased
CROFT William H		20348656	Sergeant		
DANIELS James E	Tennessee				'
DASH Walter M	Ohio				'
DAVID Raphael J	Michigan				'
DAVIS Clarence E	Kansas				'
DAVIS John T	Texas				'
DAVIS Joseph O	Indiana				'
DAVIS Leo	Illinois				'
DAVIS Robert D	Ohio				'
DAVIS Tilford A	Texas	38039255	Technician 5		'
DAVIS William	New York	42021662	Technician 5		'
DAWDY Richard E	Michigan				'
DAY Charles A Jr	New York				'
DE BELLA Martin J	California				'
DENTON Bernard A	Virginia	33042023	Corporal	4260 QM Tr Co	' (146th Corporal) deceased
DESO James A		32664666	Private		
DI DONATO Florian	Rhode Island				'
DI GIORGIO Arthur A	Ohio				'
DI SANO Benjamin F	Rhode Island	31148074	Technician 5		'
DIEHL William F	Pennsylvania	33574383	Technician 5		'
DINKFELT Clarence R	Pennsylvania				
DISNEY William G	Dist Columbia	20348657	Technician 5	146 QM Tr Co	A ' deceased
DOMINGUEZ Juan	Texas				
DORMAN Willis W	N Carolina				
DOVE Carl E	Maryland	33009155	Technician 5	1325 SCU	deceased 2d Platoon
DOVYAK Frank B	Pennsylvania	33037021	Technician 5	4267 QM Tr Co	' (146th T5 3d platoon)
DOWELL Belverd	Texas				'
DOWNEY David D	Texas				'
DUGAN Richard E	Pennsylvania				'
DUIGNAN Charles L	Ohio	35601317	Technician 5		'
DUNCAN Walter R	Virginia	20348911	Corporal	4260 QM Tr Co	C ' (146th Corporal) deceased
EBY Isaac W	Michigan				'
EDGERTON William H	Michigan				'
EDWARDS Denzel M	Indiana				'
EDWARDS Gale F	Indiana				'
ELIAS Stephen M	Ohio				'
ELLIOTT Robert J	Massachusetts				

Name	State	Number	Rank	Unit	Notes
ELLIS James C	Texas				[1]
ENDICOTT Marvin L	Missouri				[1]
FARLEY Hugh J	New York	32709799	Private		[1]
FEIST Billie J	Texas				[1]
FELDMAN Robert C	Michigan				[1]
FERRY James H		33009370	Private First Class		
FIELDS Sherman S	Texas				[1]
FINCKE Arnold A	Texas				
FISHER Emanuel S		33042026	Technician 5		deceased
FISHER Raymond L	Michigan				
FITZWATER Norman W	Missouri				[1]
FLOREY Nicola P Jr	Vermont				[1]
FONTENOT Howard B	Louisiana				[1]
FOREMAN Ruben	Illinois				[1]
FORNILL Frick R	Maryland	20348658	Sergeant	4257 QM Tr Co	A [1] deceased 2d & 3d Pltns (146th Sgt)
FORREST James W	Tennessee	34495588	Technician 5		[1]
FOSTER Grady W	Georgia	34136684	Technician 5		[1]
FOSTER Lonnie S	Mississippi				[1]
FRAZER William D	Missouri	33009164	Corporal	146 QM Tr Co	[1]
GADOW Alfred B		33009327	Technician 5	146 QM Tr Co	
GALLAGHER William	Pennsylvania				[1]
GARDNER Howard E	Kentucky				
GEE Wilson W	Virginia	33042212	Technician 5	4267 QM Tr Co	[1] deceased 2d Platoon (146th T5)
GERRAIN Orlando	New York				[1]
GIBSON Joseph C R	Kentucky				[1]
GINGRICH Richard E	Pennsylvania				[1]
GONZALEZ Jose R	Texas				
GOODWIN John W				Sergeant	A" Jack"
GRIFFIN Paul P	Tennessee	6929175	Private		[1]
GRIMES Elbert J	Dist Columbia	33450618	Private		[1]
GRISWOLD William S	Arizona				[1]
GUALTIRE Dominick	Pennsylvania				[1]
GUNNER Walter T	Illinois				[1]
HADSOCK Roscoe P	Florida	34530868	Tecnician 5		[1]
HALK Michael M	New York	32086875	Private		[1]
HALLETT William					
HAMILTON Charles R R Jr		33009362	Technician 5		maintenance
HARDING Donald				Sergeant	A
HARRIGAN Roy F	Ohio				[1]
HASHIMOTO Yasuo	California				[1]
HAYES Jack H	Tennessee				[1]
HEILMANN Charles L	Pennsylvania				[1]
HEIPLE Wilmont T	Pennsylvania				[1]
HEISERMAN Leslie E	Kansas				[1]
HENRY Donald W	West Virginia				[1]
HERRICK Arnold A	Maine				[1]
HILDEBRANDT					A
HILLEARY Paul E	West Virginia				[1]
HILTGEN Thomas C	Nebraska				[1]
HINCHLEY Noel W	Indiana				[1]
HINRICHS Frederick R	Kansas				[1]
HOBBS James R	Kentucky				[1]
HOGREFE Albert H	Illinois				[1]
HOLLETT John W	Maryland	33009332	Sergeant	146 QM Tr Co	[1]
HOLT Henry R	Virginia	13014950	Technician 5	4267 QM Tr Co	[1] (146th PFC)
HOOPES La Vere R	Arizona				
HORNSBY Charles	Indiana	6986693	Technician 5	4259 QM Tr Co	[1]
HUCK Raymond A	Missouri	37380402	Private		[1]
HUNT Reed O	Florida				[1]
INMAN Clarence S	Tennessee	34143382	Corporal	4257 QM Tr Co	[1] (146th T5)
IWANE Kenneth S	Hawaii				[1]
JANESKE Harry E	Michigan	36149900	Private		[1]
JENKINS Benedict E	Maryland	33009382	Technician 5	4267 QM Tr Co	[1] (146th T5) deceased
JENKINS Reubin W		20348660	Technician 4		
JOHNS Roy P	Indiana				[1]
JOHNSON George E	Maryland	33009257	Staff Sergeant	4257 QM Tr Co	[1] (146th Staff Sgt)
JOHNSON Walter	New York				
KASTINA Joseph Jr		33009191	Corporal	146 QM Tr Co	
KELLY August R	S Carolina				[1]

Name	State	Serial No	Rank	Unit	Notes
KENNEDY Maurice J	New Jersey				
KENNEL Fred E	Maryland	20348643	Technician 4	146 QM Tr Co	A [1] 1st Cook
KENYON Meril T	Nebraska	01703908	Second Lieutenant		[1] ex Graves Registration unit
KIMBLE Jack P	Georgia				
KISHIMOTO Harry M	Colorado				[1]
KOCH			Lieutenant		
KOMENDA William J	Dist Columbia	20348782	Private		[1]
KRIEG Harold L	Texas				[1]
KRIVZ Edward L	Minnesota	37285604	Technician 5		[1]
KROMER Roland E	Pennsylvania				[1]
LAKER Charles M	Maryland	33009265	Technician 5	4267 QM Tr Co	[1] (146th T5) deceased
LAMB Richard F		33041920	Sergeant		
LANCE William E		20348799	Private First Class		
LANG Alfred J	Maryland	33009144	Corporal		
LECHERT Frank W Jr	Maryland	33009120	Tech Sergeant	4267 QM Tr Co	[1] (146th Corporal)
LESTRANGE William F	Pennsylvania	33050995	Technician 5		[1]
LEWIS Phil					A
LIGHT Robert A	Pennsylvania	33233829	Technician 5		
LINCKS Virgil R	Arkansas	37106663	Technician 5		
LINTON Aubrey					remained in Middle East
LINTON William A		33009364	Technician 5	312 QM Sales	
LITTLE Francis E	Maryland	20348783	Sergeant	4267 QM Tr Co	[1] (146th Corporal) deceased
LOCKRIDGE James M		6958147	Private		
LONGANECKER Harry E	Ohio	35384355	Technician 5		[1]
LORENZ Herman C		33009091	Private First Class		deceased
LOUDERMELT Sylvester	N Carolina	34115151	Corporal		[1]
LOWE Edward W	Tennessee				[1]
LUCIDO Richard T	Michigan				[1]
LUTZ Oral B	Texas				[1]
LYLE James C		0-346479	Captain		F remained Mid E as Major deceased
LYON Leonard P		33009383	Technician 5		
McCLELLAND Samuel		6889188	1st Sergeant		
McDOWELL Rex K	Dist Columbia				[1]
McILWEE Glenn M		W2-124696	WOJG		A (146th Corporal, 33009294)
McINTOSH Melvin G	Oregon				
McLEMORE Eugene M			1st Sergeant		A
McMASTER William H	New York	0-1575461	1st Lieutenant		[1] deceased 147th & 146th
MACKEY Clarence J Jr	Virginia	20348959	Technician 5	146 QM Tr Co	[1] Cook/driver
MADDEN George A	Pennsylvania				
MANTOR Edward G	New York		First Sgt after 1945		[1] repl ex 82nd Airborne Div
MAROZ Louis A	New York				[1]
MARTIN Donald M	Montana				[1]
MARTIN George B	Pennsylvania				[1]
MASON Tonchie Y	Virginia	33048805	Corporal	4257 QM Tr Co	[1] (146th Cpl) deceased
MATHEWS Roland H	Dist Columbia	20348662	Technician 4	146 QM Tr Co	A [1] "Matey" deceased
MENKE Richard H	Illinois				
MILEY George E jr			2nd Lieutenant		B/A later 45th Inf
MILLER Edward H	West Virginia				[1]
MINAR Edward J	Pennsylvania				[1]
MIYAMOTO Gordon N	Arizona				[1]
MOLLER George W	Maryland	13136646	Private		[1]
MONROE Kenneth					
MOORE Alva W	Kansas				[1]
MOORE Harvey O	California				[1]
MORASCO Rosco J	New York	32094265	Technician 5		[1] joined in England
MOTOOKA Jeso	Wyoming				[1]
MYERS George K	Ohio	35592350	Private		[1]
NAGASAWA Tatsuo G	Hawaii				[1]
NAMBA Jack K	Illinois				[1]
NICHOLS Allen H		20348785	Private		
NISHIDA Shogo F	Utah				[1]
O'BRIEN Thomas O	Connecticut				[1]
O'NÉILL Michael	Indiana				[1]
OLBIK Charles J	New York				[1]
OLIVER Stuart E	Virginia	20349331	Technician 5	146 QM Tr Co	F [1] 2d Ptn "Hayshaker"
OSOWSKI Edward E	Connecticut	31102612	Private First Class		[1]
OWENS Robert F	Maryland	33009307	Staff Sergent	9768TSU	146th Coy clerk remained in ME
PACE Walter T	Texas	38230098	Technician 5		[1]
PAMCO Salvatore J	New Jersey				[1]
PAPPAS Nick G	Texas				[1]
PARKER Elijah G	Missouri	37402259	Private		[1]

Name	State	Serial No.	Rank	Unit	Notes
PARKER Henry M	S Carolina	34098313	Technician 5		[1]
PERRY Robert D	Maryland	33009330	Sergeant	4267 QM Tr Co	D [1] (Cpl 146th) deceased
PHELPS Dick					A
PHILIPS Eugene					A Bugler
PHILLIPS Bernice E		33042162	Private First Class		
PHILLIPS Stanley W			2nd Lieutenant		A
PHILLIPS Wendell C	Massachusetts				[1]
POSEY George					
POST Herbert L	New York	32352750	Private		[1]
POWELL Joel C	Georgia	34576488	Technician 5		[1] deceased joined in Middle East
PRICE Emert	West Virginia	35446958	Private		[1]
PRIEST Gaylon R		33045629	Private		[1] 2d Ptn
PROSER Milton		33001463	Private		
PRUSSACK Walter	Michigan				[1]
PURDY Harold A	Massachusetts				[1]
RANDOLPH James W	Alabama				[1]
RARICK Orville D	Michigan				[1]
RAYNOR Harold J	New York				[1]
RAYSON Foster H	Pennsylvania				[1]
RECCO John Jr	Massachusetts				[1]
RENDEAU Clarence G		20739250	Private First Class		
REYNA Genaro C	Texas				[1]
RHEA Aubrey A	Virginia	33041704	Sergeant	4260 QM Tr Co	[1] (146th Sgt) deceased
ROBERTSON Renso W	Tennessee	34041167	Technician 5		
ROYAL Robert B			Sergeant		A
RUSH Ralph C III	Pennsylvania				
RUSSELL Reginald R Jr	Dist Columbia	20348647	Staff Sergeant	146 QM Tr Co	A [1] 2d platoon
SAKAMOTO Sueo	Arizona				[1]
SANDERS Norval H	Missouri				
SANDOZ Hubert	Captain				146 & 147 remained in Middle East
SAVAGE Joseph Jr		32058802	Private		
SCHERER Wallace E		20348945	First Sergeant	4268th	(146th Sgt)
SCOTT Solomon	Maryland	33009109	Technician 5	4259 QM Tr Co	[1] (146th PFC)
SEMIK Anthony M	Ohio				[1]
SHARP William E	New York				
SHAW Albert C	Dist Columbia	20348665	Technician 5	146 QM Tr Co	A [1]
SHAW Charley	Georgia				[1]
SHELZI Louis A	Massachusetts				[1]
SHERLEY Vincent F	New York				[1]
SHIGEMOTO Denichi	Hawaii				
SHUTT Kirby J		19104321	Private		
SILLERS Daniel J		20348666	Corporal	4268 QM Tr Co	A (146th Cpl 3d Platoon)
SINCLAIR Richard M	Massachusetts	0536299	Second Lieutenant		[1]
SIPES Merrill J		33009301	Sergeant	4268 QM Tr Co	Motor Sgt deceased
SISK Frank	Georgia				[1]
SIZEMORE Lee R	Alabama				[1]
SKOBIELEW Ralph G			2nd Lieutenant	4268 QM Tr Co	joined in England
SLATER James A	Illinois				[1]
SLATER Rowland Jr	New York				[1]
SMITH Elmer R	Maryland				[1]
SNIDER George E	Indiana				[1]
SPARACINO Ralph A	Dist Columbia				A [1]
STANLEY			Lieutenant		A
STONER Norvil H	Pennsylvania	13073135	Private First Class		[1]
STRONG Virgil R	Nebraska				[1]
STRUGALA Adam C	Pennsylvania	33055102	Technician 5		[1]
STUART Harry P	Maryland	33009141	Corporal	4267 QM Tr Co	[1] (146th T5) deceased
SULLIVAN Russell W	Alabama				[1]
SVEEN Marvin O	North Dakota				[1]
SWAIM Lawrence E	Pennsylvania				
SWARTZLANDER Leroy A		35550814	Private		
SYLVESTRI Frank T	New York				[1]
TALIAFERRO Hollis V		35026005	Sergeant (4268th)		(Cpl 146th) "Tex"
TAYLOR William E	Virginia	33042125	Technician 5	4257 QM Tr Co	[1] (146th T5)
TEAGLE John W	Virginia	20348667	Technician 4	4260 QM Tr Co	[2] [1] First Cook (146th T5) deceased
THIBEAULT Charles H	Massachusetts	31077366	Technician 5		
THIBODAUX George J		34153513	Private		deceased
THOMPSON Lyman C	Michigan				[1]
THOMPSON Maynard A	Maryland				[1]
TIMLIN Stephan J	New York				[1]
TOPPEL Elroy W Jr		20349338	Technician 5		
TOYAHARA Yoshito	Arizona				[1]
TURNAGE Gordon S	Michigan				[1]

Name	State	Number	Rank	Unit	Notes
VANCE Jesse F	Missouri				[1]
VANOVER Ralph J	West Virginia				[1]
VARNER Edd S		35551107	Technician 5		
VINCE Louis Jr	Connecticut		First Lieutenant		[1]
VIRAG Paul	Ohio	35551107	Technician 5		[1]
WADDELL Thomas	West Virginia	35207680	Private		[1]
WALKER Lester E	Missouri				[1]
WALKER Murvis E	Louisiana				[1]
WALKER William N	Louisiana				[1]
WALSTON	Captain				"Bull Moose"
WALTER Stanley A	Dist Columbia	33042167	Technician 5	146 QM Tr Co	[1]
WARD Paul P	Maryland	20348794	Technician 4	4260 QM Tr Co	[1] maintenance (146th T4) deceased
WARGO Walter E	Pennsylvania				[1]
WARREN James S		34135700	Private First Class		[1]
WARVIN Jesse A		20348672	Technician 5		A maintenance deceased
WATSON William J	Minnesota				[1]
WEBER Rudolph Jr	Pennsylvania	33081947	Technician 5		A [1]
WEEKS Kennon					not overseas
WELCH Bob			Sergeant		A deceased
WELCH Jim					A
WELLS Robert W	Michigan	16010642	Corporal		[1]
WENDLER William E					deceased
WERNER Livingston P	New York	32810601	Private		[1]
WHITE Donald C	Ohio				[1]
WHITE William C	Massachusetts				[1]
WHITEMAN Marlin R	Pennsylvania	33017734	Corporal		[1] deceased
WIENER Milton	New York				[1]
WILKINSON William V		20348960	Technician 5		C
WILLMAN Paul A		6943289	Private		
WILSON Russell E	California	10675041	Private		[1]
YAFFE Abraham		33041922	Private		3d Platoon
YOUNG Robert					A
ZEMEL Michael	Maryland	33009133	Technician 5	4260 QM Tr Co	[1] Draftee, 2d Ptn (146th T5)
ZUPPARDI Frank Jr		32069227	Private First Class		

APPENDIX C

World War II Stations
146th Quartermaster Truck Company

8.2.41	- 14.9.41	= Fort George G. Meade, Maryland
18.9.41	- 25.9.41	= AP Hill Military Reservation, Virginia
29.9.41	- 7.12.41	= North Carolina Maneuver Area
9.12.41	- 28.4.42	= Fort Meade
12.3.42		= 146th QM Truck Company created
28.4.42	- 8.6.42	= Indiantown Gap Military Reservation, Pennsylvania
8.6.42	- 27.8.42	= Fort Meade
28.8.42	- 11.9.42	= Charleston, South Carolina
12.9.42	- 21.9.42	= Fort Dix, New Jersey
21.9.42	- 31.10.42	= at sea (ss Aquitania)
31.10.42		= Massawa, Eritrea *
1943	- early	= stationed by platoon: 1st at Tripoli Base Command
		2nd at Benghazi Base Command
		3rd at Heliopolis Depot, Egypt
1943	- late	= 3rd Platoon at Tel-a-Viv, Palestine
		Coy Hq at Benghazi
1.11.43	- 27.2.44	= Camp Russell B. Huckstep, Egypt
1.3.44	- 17.3.44	= at sea (ss Otranto)
18.3.44	- 16.4.44	= Southampton, England
13.4.44		= Charlton Marshall,Dorset
16.4.44	- 2.6.44	= Dorchester, England
2.6.44	- 13.7.44	= Bristol, England
13.7.44	- 14.7.44	= Marshalling Area "C", England
15.7.44	- 16.7.44	= at sea
16.7.44		= APO 113, France
17.7.44	- 21.7.44	= Area T-453, France
21.7.44	- 29.7.44	= St Pierre du Mont, France
29.7.44	- 21.8.44	= Auville, France
11.8.44		= Reorganised as 146th QM Truck Co (Heavy)
21.8.44	- 28.8.44	= Treviers, France
28.8.44	- 10.9.44	= Alencon, France
10.9.44	- 11.9.44	= Cherisy, France
11.9.44	- 19.9.44	= Dreux, France
19.9.44	- 1.11.44	= Trappes, France
1.11.44	- 27.1.45	= St Etienne du Rouvray, France
27.1.45	- 3.3.45	= Ghent, Belgium
3.3.45	- 1.4.45	= Mons, Belgium
1.4.45	- 5.4.45	= Adendorf, Germany
5.4.45	- 9.4.45	= Bergheim, Germany
9.4.45	- 10.4.45	= Nechenheim, Germany
10.4.45	- 26.5.45	= Berkum, Germany
26.5.45	- 15.6.45	= Duren, Germany
15.6.45	- 1.7.45	= Munchen Gladbach, Germany
2.7.45	- 6.7.45	= Halle, Germany
6.7.45	- 10.2.46	= Berlin, Germany
9.2.46		= Inactivated

* This was indeed the destination, but for reasons explained in the text, the 146th never arrived.
** Source = U.S. Army Center of Military History.

APPENDIX D

CAMPAIGN AND OCCUPATION CREDITS
146th QM TRUCK COMPANY

CAMPAIGN DATES

"Egypt - Libya"   = 11th June 1942 to 12th February 1943
"Normandy"   = 6th June 1944 to 24th July 1944
"Northern France"   = 25th July 1944 to 14th September 1944
"Rhineland"   = 15th September 1944 to 21st March 1945
"Ardennes - Alsace" = 16th December 1944 to 25th January 1945
"Central Europe"   = 22nd March 1945 to 11th May 1945

Source = U.S. Army Center of Military History

146th CAMPAIGN CREDITS

Ardennes-Alsace
Central Europe
Normandy
Northern France
Rhineland

Source = U.S. Army Center of Military History

146th CAMPAIGN CREDITS

Ardennes - Alsace
Central Europe
Northern France
Rhineland
Germany (occupation credit)

Source = Unit Citation & Campaign participation credit register

---

PERSONAL CAMPAIGN CREDITS

Ardennes
Egypt - Libya
Normandy
Northern France
Rhineland

Source = Bill Albright discharge papers.

DERORATIONS & CITATIONS

American Campaign Medal
European African Middle Eastern
(with 5 Battle Stars)
World War II Victory Medal

PERSONAL CAMPAIGN CREDITS

Egypt- Libya
Normandy
Northern France
Rhineland
Tunisia

Source = Linnie L. Baker discharge papers

DECORATIONS & CITATIONS

American Defense Medal
European African Middle Eastern Service Medal
Good Conduct Medal

PERSONAL CAMPAIGN CREDITS

Ardennes
Central Europe
Egypt - Libya
Normandy
Northern France
Rhineland

Source = Edward G. Blue discharge papers

DECORATIONS & CITATIONS

American Defense Medal
European African Middle Eastern Service Medal
Good Conduct Medal

PERSONAL CAMPAIGN CREDITS

Ardennes
Central Europe
Egypt - Libya
Normandy
Northern France
Rhineland

Source = Dennis W. Cheeley discharge papers

DECORATIONS & CITATIONS

American Defense Medal
European African Middle Eastern Service Medal

PERSONAL CAMPAIGN CREDITS

Ardennes
Central Europe
Normandy
Northern France
Rhineland

Source = Joseph Corrao discharge papers

DECORATIONS & CITATIONS

European African Middle Eastern Theater Ribbon
(with 1 Silver Battle Star)
World War II victory Medal
Good Conduct Medal

PERSONAL CAMPAIGN CREDITS

Egypt - Libya
Normandy
Northern France
Rhineland

Source = Frederick H Cox discharge papers

DECORATIONS & CITATIONS

American Campaign Medal
American Defense Service Medal
Drivers Medal
European African Middle Eastern Service Medal
Good Conduct Medal
World War II Victory Medal

PERSONAL CAMPAIGN CREDITS

Egypt - Libya
Normandy
Northern France
Rhineland

Source = John M. Crandall discharge papers.

DECORATIONS & CITATIONS

American Defense Service Medal
European African Middle Eastern Service Medal

PERSONAL CAMPAIGN CREDITS

Egypt - Libya
Tunisia

Source = Carl E. Dove discharge papers

DECORATIONS & CITATIONS

American Defense Service Medal
European African Middle Eastern Service Medal
(with 2 Bronze Battle Stars)

PERSONAL CAMPAIGN CREDITS

DECORATIONS & CITATIONS

American Defense Service Medal
European African Middle Eastern Service Medal
Good Conduct Medal

Source = William A. Linton discharge papers

PERSONAL CAMPAIGN CREDITS

DECORATIONS & CITATIONS

American Defense Service Medal
European African Middle Eastern Service Medal
Good Conduct Medal

Source = Robert F. Owen discharge papers

PERSONAL CAMPAIGN CREDITS

Ardennes
Central Europe
Normandy
Northern France
Rhineland

Source = Robert D. Perry discharge Papers

DECORATIONS & CITATIONS

American Defence Service Medal
European African Middle Eastern Service Medal
Good Conduct Medal

PERSONAL CAMPAIGN CREDITS

Ardennes
Central Europe
Normandy
Northern France
Rhineland

DECORATIONS & CITATIONS

American Defense Service Medal
European African Middle Eastern Service Medal
(with 5 Bronze Stars)
Good Conduct Medal

Source = Rudolph Weber Jr discharge papers

Wins Commendation

Corporal Rudolph Weber, a son of Mrs Louisa Weber of 150 Oak Street, has been commended by headquarters of the Communications Zone of the Army in Belgium, for his part in operations of the 146th Quartermaster Truck Co. which exceeded by half the regular shipping quota during a two month period. The mission of his company was 24,000 ton-miles a day, a ton-mile being one ton transported one mile. The commendation by Major General Frank S. Ross reads: 'At a time when transportation facilities are critically strained I wish to express my appreciation of the fine work done by the 146th Quartermaster Truck Co. for the superior manner in which they have maintained vital transport'.

APPENDIX E

Vehicles

Miltary vehicles of World War II were divided and sub-divided into various groups. The primary division was between administrative and tactical vehicles. Administrative vehicles were generally commercial types that were not required to meet military specifications, and tactical vehicles were specifically designed or adapted to meet military criteria for use in combat areas.

Tactical vehicles were sub-divided into General Purpose Vehicles - designed to be used either for the movement of personnel, supplies, ammunition and equipment, or for the towing of guns, trailers or semi- trailers, or into Special Equipment Vehicles - which were basically identical but fitted with special purpose bodywork or equipment.

U.S. Army vehicles were usually painted a semi-gloss olive drab and issued with a registration number that was displayed on both sides of the engine hood and on the rear of the body.

This was prefixed by the letter "W" that indicated a War Department vehicle and the first or first two digits of the registration number indicated the vehicle type, the following digits indicated the sequence in which the vehicle was added to the type group.

OO Trucks, maintenance
2   Trucks, light, ½ to 1 ton (pickup, panel etc)
20   Trucks, recce, and buses
3   Trucks, medium 1½ ton (cargo, dump, truck-tractor)
4   Trucks, light-heavy, 2½ ton, and up to 4-5 ton
5   Trucks, heavy, and prime movers, 5 ton and over
50   Trucks, fire (fire and crash), all sizes
8   Tractors, wheeled (light, medium, heavy)

The 146th Quartermaster Truck Company were originally issued with what was commonly known as " GMC 6 x 6's " or "Jimmy's". These were six wheeled trucks produced by various plants of the General Motors Corporation to U.S. Army specification G 508 and was probably the most widely used transport vehicle of World War II, over half a million being produced by the end of 1945.

The design and development of this "workhorse of the Army" had been carried out by the Motor Transport Division of the Quartermaster Corps culminating in a specification to suit all arms.

The GMC model designation of CCKWX-353-120 was of a 2½ ton cargo truck powered by a GMC 270, six cylinder 269.5 cubic inch engine through a five speed gearbox, plus reverse, with a transfer box to double the number of gears available. A wheelbase of 164 inches gave an overall size of 256" x 88" x 110", and an unladen weight of 10,350 lbs.

They had metal cabs with hinged windshields, and a few of the 146th' vehicles had front mounted winches. The bodies were standard cargo design of steel construction with tip-up wood slatted troop seats, metal bows and canvas covers.

In 1944 when the 146th converted to tractor / trailers, they were given International KR-11, 5 ton tractors built to U.S. Army specification G 542. The IHC 'Red Diamond' 451 cu.in. engine was ideally suited to long distance haulage through a transmission of 5 forward and one reverse gears, air brakes and 11.00 - 20 tyres. They had a canvas cab over the engine and were matched with 10 ton 36' semi trailers with 4' high sides and canvas covers and carried a forty gallon fuel tank under each side of the body.

INDEX